GW01388361

...NING AND TIDYING AROUND THE FLAT DOING THIS WILL MAKE YO...

...ONSIDER HAVING A MIXT...

...ENDERS IN YOUR FLAT -

it works best

...H IT?

BE UPFRONT WITH YOUR ...ATTIES

SET UP A JOINT FLAT ACCOUNT FOR THE RENT TO COME OUT OF.

do the dishes when you finish eating to save disputes

before eating ...eones food

...spective before

DON'T SCREW THE CREW

KEEP YOUR ROOM AS MESSY AS YOU LIKE

IF YOU ARE A GUEST AT SOMEONE...
FLAT, OFFER TO CONTRIBUTE...

DON'T IT WILL GO BLUE LEAVE FOOD OUT

KEEP YOUR MANNERS IN CHECK

...K

...F INCLUDE YOURSELF

...IN FLAT ...CTIVITIES

DON'T MEASURE THE ROOMS INCH FOR INCH AND DIVIDE UP THE RENT ACCORDINGLY

CONSIDER FLAT-TING WITH RAN-DOMS AS IT CAN BROADEN YOUR FRIEND CIRCLES

DON'T BITCH BEHIND YOUR FLATTIES BACK

COMMUNICATE

...NS TAKE YOUR VALUABLES ...THE ...ER. YOU LEAVE THE FLAT FOR A LONG PERIOD OF ...NIT TIME

don't tweet about your flatmates when you are in a fig... because chances are they will see it and it's rather lame!

GO INTO YOUR FLAT WITH RE... ISTIC EXPECT... TIONS!

DO SOME HONEST RESEARCH ON WHO YOU INTEND TO MOVE IN WITH, SCOPE THEIR FACEBOOKS, TWITTER OR ASK PREVIOUS FLATTIES IF THEY CAN SHED SOME LIGHT

DON'T BE A PRIC...

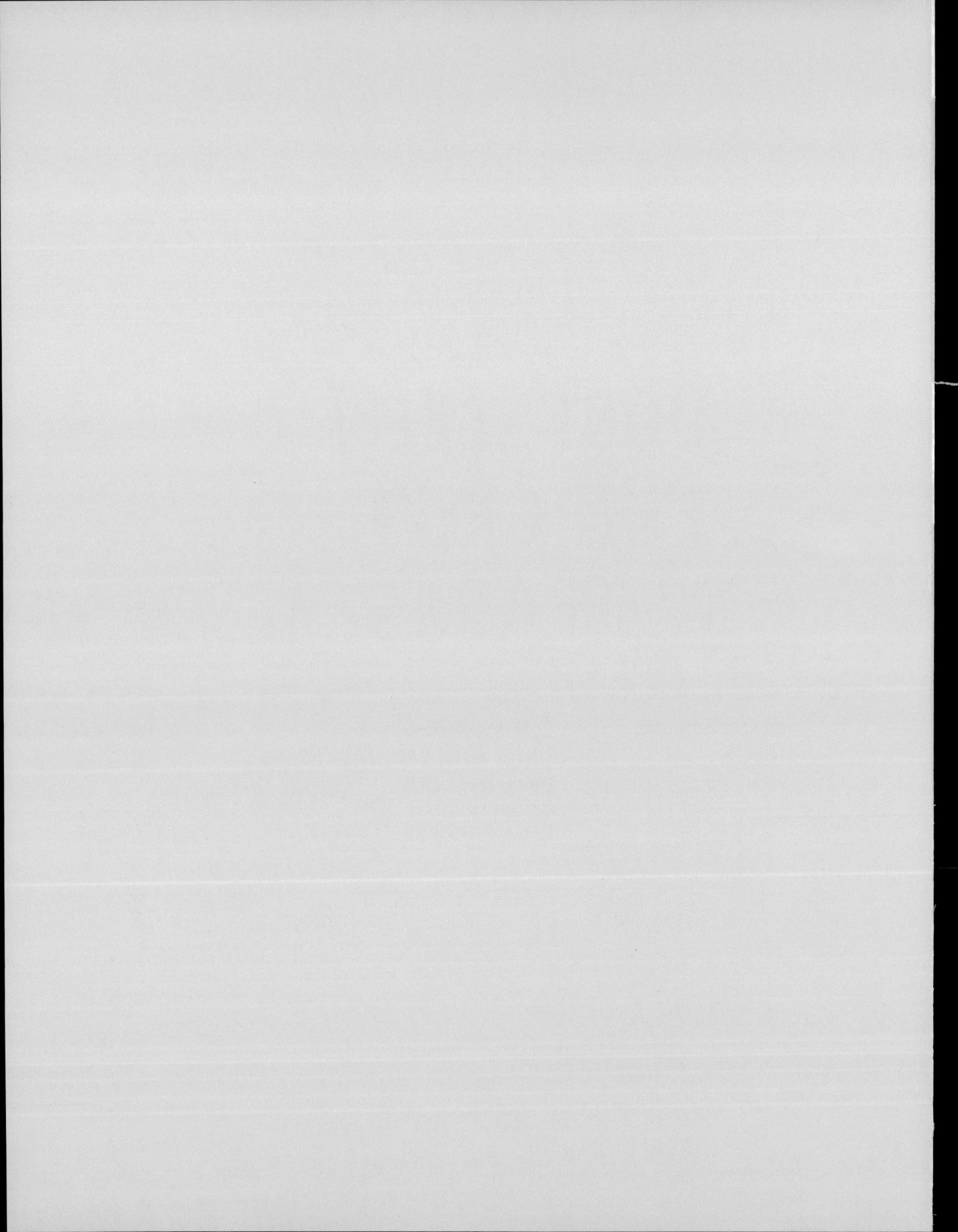

LAUREN EARL

—

Flatter's
Survival Guide

—

AWA PRESS

LAUREN EARL

—

Flatter's
Survival Guide

CONTENTS

DO YOUR
Bloody dishes
We are over it!!!!

Emma is passed out
on the bathroom floor.
Please check on her occasionally.

INTRO-
DUC-
TION

FLAT

THIS ONE

1. AN APARTMENT THAT YOU RENT
WEEKLY OR MONTHLY.
2. SOMEONE WHO IS NOT COOL AND IS DULL
AND BORING.
3. A WOMAN WITH SMALL BREASTS.
4. SOMETHING THAT IS LEVEL—DOES
NOT INCREASE OR DECREASE.
5. THE NAME GIVEN TO SOMETHING FILLED
WITH AIR THAT IS NOW DEFLATED.

So, you have decided to go flatting—that's great! You are about to embark on the best time of your life! No more chores or rules to follow, no more nagging from your parents, just epic parties and complete freedom. You can replace siblings with friends, dinner parties with dance parties, and even your breakfast with pizza. Everything is going to be your way from here on out, right?

Before you go rushing out the door, be warned: you may soon discover that mum's home-cooked roast never sounded better and those unexpected bills piling up fling you right back to reality.

This book will take you through the various stages of flatting, from planning to move in, all the way through to moving out again. It will answer the tough questions, such as how to avoid eating two-minute noodles every night because your parents aren't paying for the groceries. It will help you choose the right flatmates so you're not stuck with people who will make you want to rip your hair out. And more importantly, because not everyone is perfect and conflicts WILL arise—even between friends—this *Flatter's Survival Guide* will show you how to establish boundaries and agreements that will prevent flat dramas.

Within these pages you'll read about real-life situations and get advice from flatters who've been there. You may even pick up some handy household etiquette and learn ways to make it up to your flatmates for peeing in the kitchen sink.

To readers who haven't been flatting yet: lucky you. Reading this book in advance will ensure you are prepared for all the exciting times ahead. Good luck!

DEAR TRACY
I HAD SEX IN YOUR BED.
SORRY ABOUT THAT.
DON'T USE YOUR PILLOW.

THE NOTES IN THIS BOOK WERE SUPPLIED BY FLATTERS FROM AROUND THE WORLD.

'WHEN I WENT FLATTING I WENT ON THE **FATKINS DIET.** I DIDN'T LOSE WEIGHT BUT I HAD A GREAT TIME!'

—

Female, 21
Palmerston North

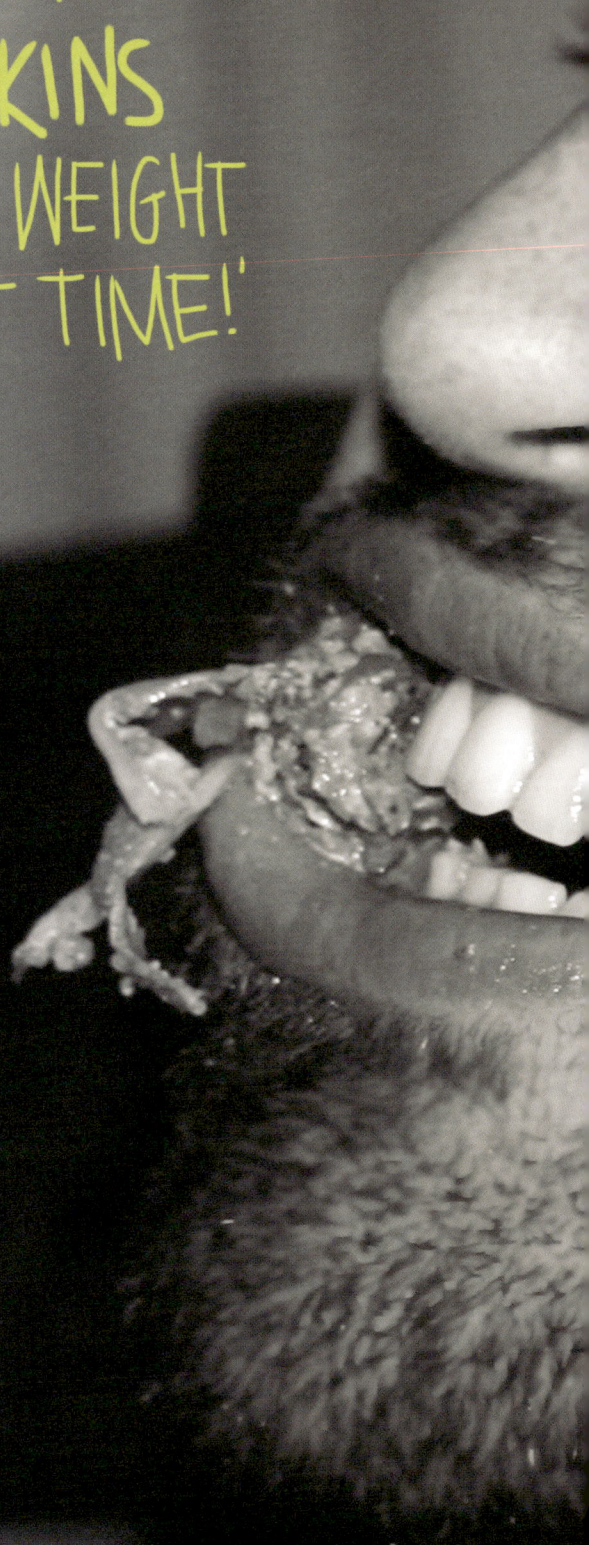

PRE
RAT

EPA-
PA-
TION

GOING FLATTING CAN BE A BIT
OF A MISSION, INVOLVING LOTS
OF TIME, EFFORT AND MONEY.
CAREFUL PLANNING WILL ENSURE
NONE OF THIS IS WASTED.

ARE YOU SURE YOU'RE READY?

SO YOU'RE THINKING OF GOING FLATTING? CRAZY FOOL!

DISHES FOR
AFRICA

UNTRUSTWORTHY
FLATMATES

ROOKIE

STEALING TOILET PAPER
FOR THE FLAT

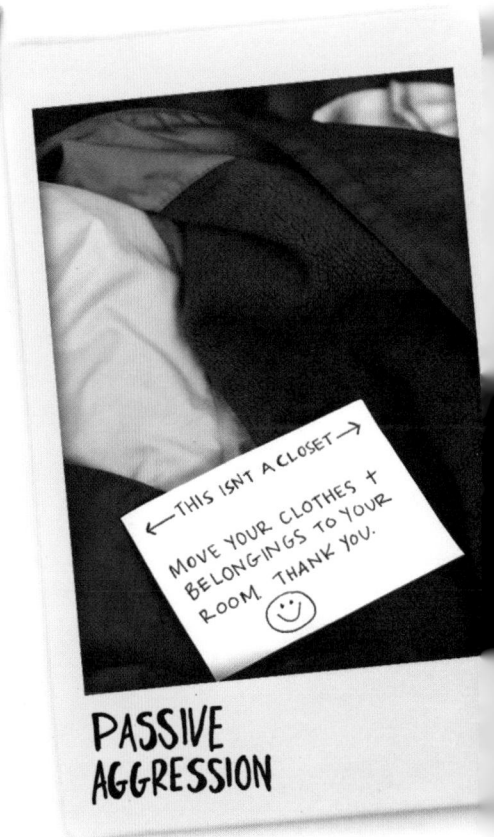

←THIS ISN'T A CLOSET→

←MOVE YOUR CLOTHES +
BELONGINGS TO YOUR
ROOM. THANK YOU.
☺

PASSIVE
AGGRESSION

Prepare yourself for
a range of interesting
flatting situations.

Let's face it—your life so far has probably been pretty cruisy. There's been food in the pantry, insulation in the walls, and maybe even a car in the garage that you can borrow to visit your friends. Going flatting means giving this up, quite possibly for a damp flat with paper-thin walls, baked-bean dinners, and homicidal flatmates. Are you really ready for this? If you answer yes to most of these questions, you should be good to go.

LIMITED SUPPLIES

01

Do I turn over a steady income?

This is your number one priority, as without it you are almost certainly doomed. It could be a stable job or a student loan, but however the money comes it needs to be enough to cover all your costs, with a rainy day fund up your sleeve for emergencies.

02

Can I really afford the rent and bills?

Rent is just part of the picture. Power, internet, food, and many other expenses will all add up. Only an accurate budget will show you whether your plan is realistic. And blowing that budget will send you straight back to where you came from.

03

Have I got what I need to go flatting?

From clean towels in the linen cupboard to the jug for your midnight Milo—your home up till now has been equipped with many necessities and comforts you may have been taking for granted. You're going to need to get your own, whether you beg, borrow or buy them.

04

Am I emotionally ready to leave the nest?

Feelings of insecurity are natural when living arrangements change, not just for people leaving home or a hostel but for anyone moving house. Think carefully about whether you can handle this big step: it might be better to wait, if that's possible, until you feel sufficiently strong and able to cope with the challenges to come.

05

Am I willing to make sacrifices?

Being responsible for yourself invariably involves sacrifices, like paying the power bill instead of buying new jeans, or nipping home for cheese on toast instead of chowing down on takeaways. Unless you're one of the lucky ones with a lottery win up your sleeve, it will pay to get used to stricter spending habits, and learning to live without luxuries.

06

Can I live with other people?

Moving in with others may be the only way to make the flat financials add up. Choosing flatmates carefully will help avoid any troubles, as will patience and tolerance all round. But if you really can't handle someone else's slurping, burping or leaving the toilet seat up, you may have to go it alone.

MUM'S LIST

NAG NAG NAG

Dishes ☑
Washing ☑
Vacuuming ☑
All cleaning ☑

HAVING YOUR PARENTS TO ANSWER BACK TO

LIVING AT THE OLDS

→ SOME OF THE THINGS FLATTERS MISS OR HATE ABOUT LIVING AT HOME:

CLOTHES

WASHED

FOLD -ED

NAG NAG NAG NAG

" WAKE UP "

AND DO SOMETHING WITH YOUR LIFE

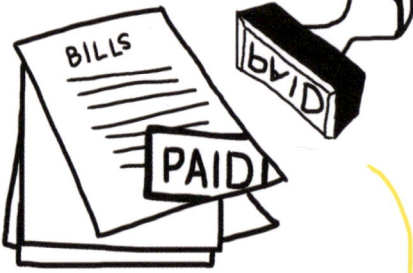

BILLS

PAID

PAID

NAG NAG NAG

$ HAVING A $ DISPOSABLE INCOME $

'TAKE THE RUBBISH OUT!'

PARENTS' DINNER PARTIES

~home-cooked~ ROASTS = + LEFT OVERS FOR LUNCHES

COSY FIREPLACE WARM ELECTRIC BLANKET

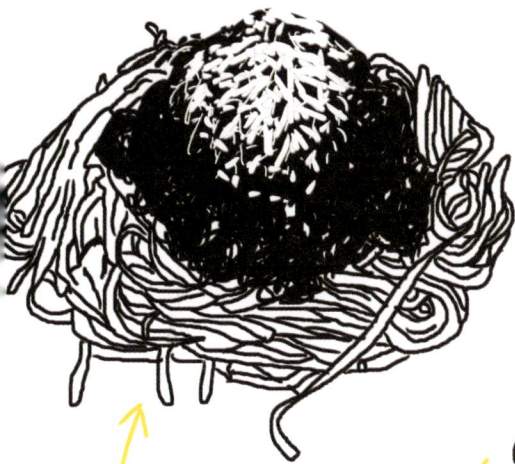

BUYING THE **BUDGET** RANGE

Sleeping all day long ZZZZZ ZZZZZZZZZZ

LIVING AT THE FLAT

→ SOME MENTIONABLE FLATTING COMPARISONS.

FUN **PARTIES**!!!

SNUGGIES FOR **WARMTH**

DISHES THAT KEEP STACKING UP

AND NOTES TELLING YOU TO DO THEM.

WASHING PILE THE SIZE OF MT RUAPEHU

HOW DEEP IS YOUR POCKET?

ELEVEN TYPICAL COSTS TO INCLUDE IN YOUR FLATTING BUDGET.

At one time or another most flatters struggle to juggle their money and keep on top of the bills. Drawing up a realistic budget will show you how much money you need each week or month to meet your financial commitments. Unexpected and often unpleasant surprises are sure to crop up, but you'll be in a much better position to handle these if you've already got the main bases covered.

01

Bond

Usually the equivalent of four weeks' rent, a bond is levied by landlords as a safeguard against any property damage or missed rent. Your bond is held in trust by the Department of Building and Housing, and when you eventually move out it will be returned to you in full—unless of course your flat-warming party results in holey walls and cigarette burns in the carpet. Or you miss rent. There's an incentive for you!

02

Rent

Your biggest weekly expense will be your rent. Whether it's to be paid weekly, fortnightly or monthly, an automatic payment will ensure that it's always paid on time and traceable. Make sure the landlord gives you a receipt if you pay it in cash. You will be asked to pay up to two weeks' rent in advance when you first move in.

03

Set-up costs

If you are moving into an established flat you will probably only have to kit out your room, but if you're setting up a new flat, get ready to invest in kitchenware, appliances, furniture, and stuff you haven't even thought of yet. You can find ideas for keeping these costs down on page 075.

04

Food

Prepare yourself for a reality check if you've never had to fork out for your own food. Splitting cooking duties and the grocery bill often proves the most economical, but you can always share some meals and look after yourself at other times. Either way, smart flatters shop mainly at low-cost supermarkets and produce markets rather than buying bits and bobs from the dairy or deli.

05

Household necessities

There are other household necessities beyond the food bill, such as cleaning products, toilet paper, rubbish bags and lightbulbs. The easiest way to cover this is by setting up a joint flat account for common household expenses, with each member paying in a small amount every week, fortnight or month.

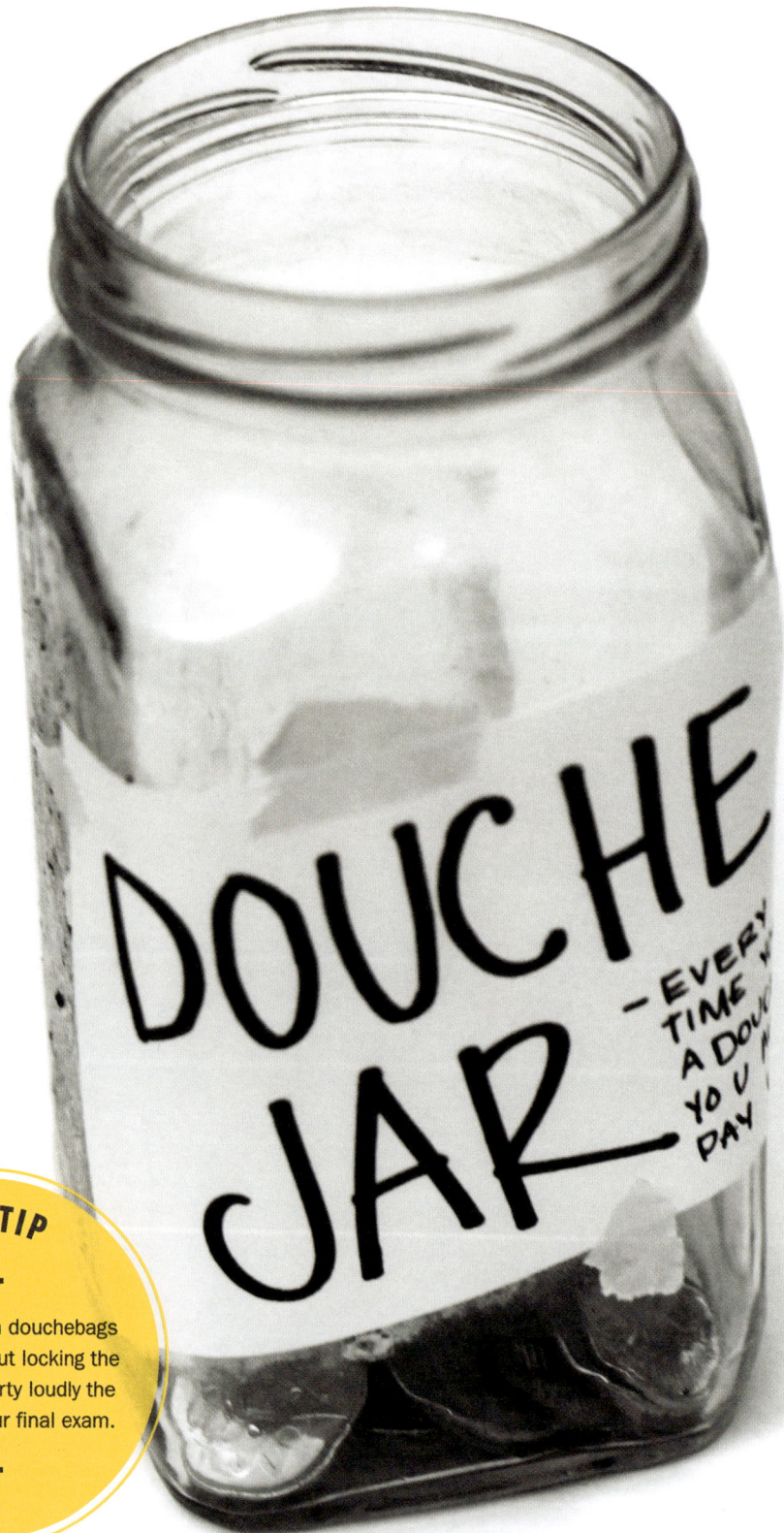

DOUCHE JAR

— EVERY
TIME
A DOU
YO U
DAY

TOP TIP

—

Impose fines on douchebags
who leave without locking the
front door or party loudly the
night before your final exam.

—

06

Electricity

Most rental agreements require you to set up and pay your own electricity account, with bills usually due monthly. The usual procedure is to divide it evenly between flatmates, but you may decide to split it another way if someone is clearly using more power than everyone else. After all, it's only fair that the person who blasts their bedroom heater night and day all winter long pays more, right?

07

Water

In towns and cities where the water supply is metered, your rental agreement will usually stipulate that the cost of water is included in your rent. Either way, make sure you know who is responsible for this bill before you sign the lease.

08

Internet

Even on a generous data plan, internet access should prove cost-effective if shared between flatmates. Avoid disputes by being honest about your usage, especially if large file downloads are likely to exceed the data allowance. Some internet providers also allow each flatmate to be billed separately, which is a sure-fire way of avoiding disputes.

09

Telephone

The landline telephone bill often proves the most disputed of household bills. Making all your calls through your cellphone or Skype will eliminate this cost altogether, but if you do share a landline you might like to set up a system where each flatmate receives their own pin number, which they need to enter before making a call. This can be arranged by contacting your local phone company.

10

Pay TV/Sky

You may decide this is one of life's luxuries you can do without, or that investing in Freeview is a satisfactory option. If you do subscribe to a pay TV service, however, make sure everyone has agreed on how the bill will be split and who will pay for any extras such as sports channels or movies.

11

Other expenses

If you can cover all these costs you're doing pretty well, but there's more—just you wait. Contents insurance, bus fares, doctor's visits and buying new socks are just some of the other things you'll need to budget for. If there's money left over after this, you could even have a night down at the pub or enjoy some greasy takeaways. Hooray!

TOP TIP

—

Learning some basic cookery
skills can avoid all sorts of
unpleasant culinary accidents.

—

I cook using the four
food groups: ~~DAIRY~~
~~MEAT~~ CANNED FROZEN
BAGGED ~~GRAINS~~ BOXED
~~FRUIT AND VEG~~

*Male, 23
Wellington*

GEAR-ING UP TO GO

THIS ISN'T A HOLIDAY—IT'S THE START OF THE REST OF YOUR LIFE.

Personal Inventory

Up to this point in life you've probably amassed a bedroom's worth of possessions, but chances are this doesn't include a bucket, a mop and a toilet brush. On page 078 we provide a list of furniture and equipment you'll need to find and share between your flatmates. Here, however, is a list that's all about you.

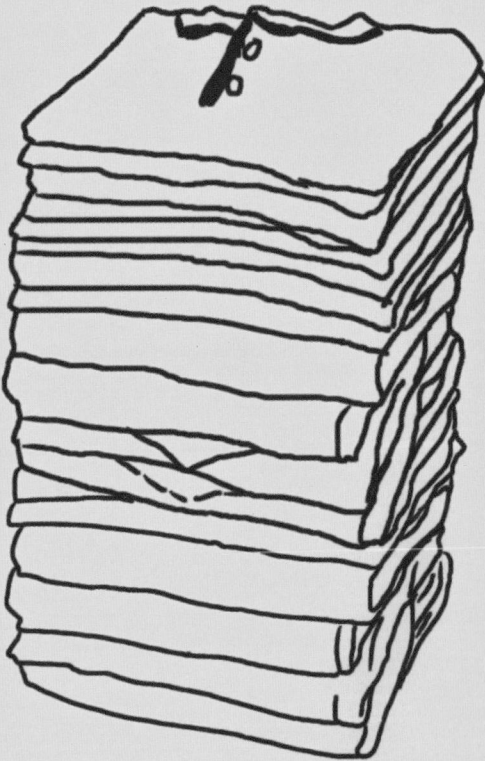

- [ ] bed & mattress
- [ ] sheets & towels
- [ ] bedside table
- [ ] reading lamp
- [ ] alarm clock
- [ ] chest of drawers
- [ ] clothes rack
- [ ] coat hangers
- [ ] mirror
- [ ] desk
- [ ] rubbish bin
- [ ] cellphone & charger
- [ ] headphones
- [ ] computer, desktop or laptop
- [ ] printer
- [ ] ink cartridge
- [ ] camera
- [ ] music player/speakers
- [ ] multi-plug
- [ ] extension cord
- [ ] surge protector
- [ ] backpack
- [ ] suitcase
- [ ] clothing for all occasions
- [ ] accessories
- [ ] shoes
- [ ] hairdryer
- [ ] toiletries
- [ ] toilet paper

- [ ] sports equipment
- [ ] games
- [ ] bike, skateboard, scooter or car
- [ ] earplugs
- [ ] torch
- [ ] sewing kit
- [ ] smoke detector
- [ ] keys

**And don't forget all your
important documents!**

- [ ] bank cards
- [ ] driver licence
- [ ] qualifications & other certificates
- [ ] insurance documents
- [ ] passport
- [ ] THIS BOOK!

FREE

HOW TIME IS SPENT WHEN PACKING TO GO FLATTING

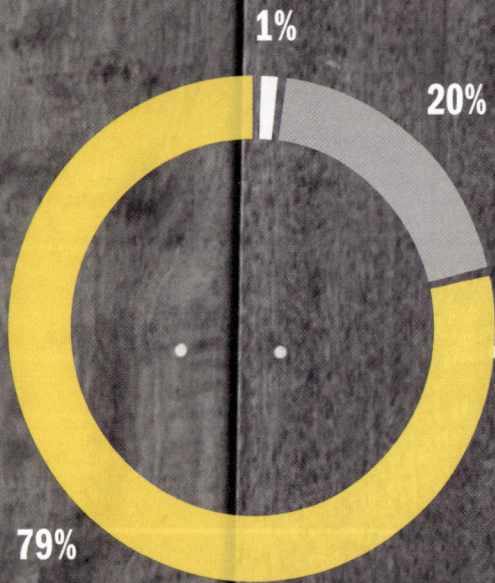

1%

20%

79%

- PACKING
- COMPLAINING
- PLAYING WITH STUFF
  YOU HAPPEN TO FIND

Results from a survey of 100 flatters.

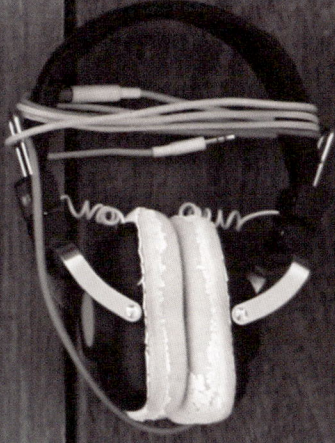

FLA
HUN

IT

CREATE A GOOD SITUATION FROM THE GET-GO BY CHOOSING THE RIGHT FLAT—AND THE RIGHT PEOPLE TO SHARE IT WITH.

FRIENDS OR RAN- DOMS?

'FLATMATES ARE FAMILY YOU CHOOSE'.

Female, 23
Wellington

WHO ARE YOU GOING TO LIVE WITH?

Unless you've decided to live alone, it's time to start looking for flatmates. Your first consideration will be whether you can—or even want to—live with friends. It might seem the obvious thing to do, but sometimes it's simply not possible or desirable. Think about the sort of people you want to live with. You might just find that the friend you move in with becomes your enemy, or that well-chosen stranger soon becomes your friend.

Living with friends

Where there's friendship, there's communication and trust, both keys to successful cohabitation. But just because your friend is fun doesn't mean they'll make a good flatmate. Take a closer look at their habits: is their bedroom a pigsty, do they waste money, are they reliable? Do they have character traits that you find irritating? Chances are these could become major factors once you move in together, and in the worst-case scenario you could be heading for a fight. Do you think your friendship would survive?

Living with strangers

The most successful flatting situations are those in which people share similar lifestyles, common interests, and the same intentions and expectations. There are plenty of people out there that you could mesh with, you just have to find them. The key is to look in the right place and ask the right questions. Can you imagine living with this person and seeing them every day?

Guys, girls or both

Among the many pros and cons of single-sex and mixed flats are the level of household cleanliness and even tempers all month round. Different combinations work for different people, but the important thing is that your flat mix is comfortable for you. Some studies have shown that interpersonal flatting problems are less prevalent in mixed flats—suggesting that men and women bring out the best in each other. Who knew?

How many flatmates?

You may be tempted to try and cram all your friends under one roof for the fun of it, but think carefully when deciding how many people you want to live with. Don't expect peace and quiet in a six-bedroom flat, but if you're a sociable person this may be your dream scenario.

TOP TIP

Moving in with like-minded strangers is a great way to make friends in a new city.

FLAT DRAMAS
BY GENDER

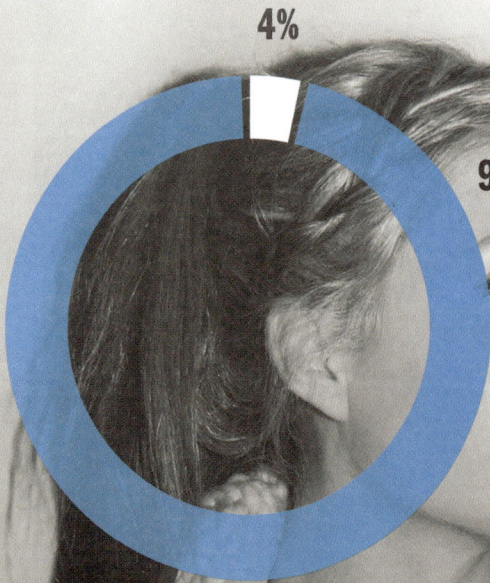

4%

96%

DRAMA IN MIXED GENDER FLATS

DRAMA IN SAME GENDER FLATS

*Results from a survey
of 100 flatters.*

'I SUPPOSE I SHOULD HAVE KNOWN THAT LIVING WITH FIVE GIRLS IN A ONE-BEDROOM FLAT WAS A RECIPE FOR DRAMA.' — *Female, 23 Wellington*

VIEW-ING

A

ROOM

CHECKING OUT AN
ESTABLISHED FLAT?
DO YOUR RESEARCH!

Viewing established flats

Being interviewed for a room in an established flat can be nerve-wracking. It pays to remember, though, that you're checking out your prospective flatmates as much as they're checking you out. As well as inspecting the room and other areas of the house, keep your ears and eyes wide open — clues to the day-to-day living arrangements are everywhere.

01

The bedroom

This will be your sanctuary, so make sure it's not only big enough, but is comfortable, too. Assess the wardrobe or other storage options. If possible, compare it to the other rooms in the house so you can gauge whether the rent is being split fairly.

02

Communal areas

Ideally there will be at least a couple of communal areas so there's room to spread out. Tensions are bound to arise in cramped conditions, or flats with too many inhabitants and not enough bathroom facilities.

03

Tidiness

It's reasonable to expect neat and tidy conditions when you visit a prospective flat. If they haven't made the effort now, they probably never do. Be suspicious of closed doors and dodgy-looking cupboards—who knows what they have hiding in there?

04

Cleanliness

Neat and tidy is relatively easy; clean is a whole different matter. Just because you're new to flatting doesn't mean you need to live with grime. Don't be afraid to peer into the corners, *discreetly,* and ask about the flat cleaning arrangements.

05

Warmth & light

The atmosphere in the house will probably tell the tale, but be sure to ask about insulation and heating, and look for any signs of mould or mildew. Also try and assess the amount of natural light, particularly if you tend to get gloomy without it.

06

Outdoor areas

If you're the sort of person who needs air-dried laundry, a vege patch and regular shots of sunshine, make a point of checking out any outside area, be it a patio, deck or garden.

07

Security & parking

Check out the door locks and window latches, and feel free to ask about the neighbours and the general vibe of the local area. Ask, too, about the parking situation if you own a vehicle or have frequent visitors who do.

08

Bitches, boozers & bohemians

Do the people in the flat seem friendly, to you and towards one another? Or do you sense disharmony or an edge of aggression? Does it look like a house of fun or a quiet retreat? There are clues everywhere, from recycling bins sporting half the stock of a liquor store, to the yoga DVD next to the television. What sort of social scene are you looking for?

Questions to ask when viewing a room

Looking around a flat will tell you only so much about the way it functions. To find out what really goes on, ask plenty of questions at the interview.

- Why are you/is the other flatmate moving out?

- How many people live here on a permanent basis?

- What do they study or do for a living?

- Who is responsible for the lease?

- What's the landlord like?

- What other flat expenses are there and how much are they?

- Is there a cleaning roster?

- Are there any house rules? If so, what are they?

- What are the food and shopping arrangements?

- Do lots of friends come over, and if so for dinners, or parties, or what?

- Do the people living here prefer to stay at home or go out?

- Is there any furniture in the room?

- When will the room be available?

- How long is the room available for and when does the lease run out?

TOP TIP

—

Look for any notes posted
around, as they can be a sign of
passive-aggressive flatmates.

—

HOW DO YOU FEEL AFTER MAKING THAT HASTY DECISION TO MOVE IN?

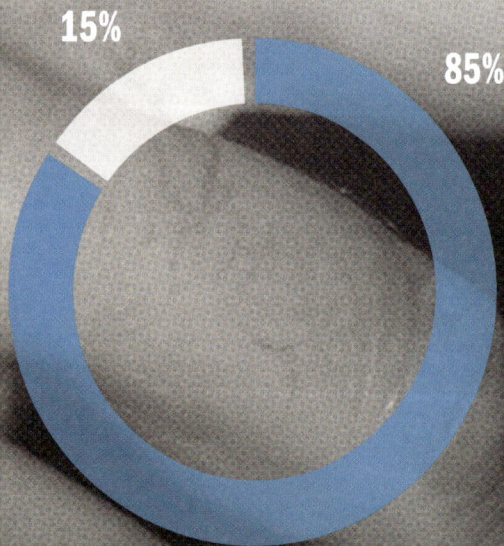

15%

85%

- AS HAPPY AS LARRY
- PRETTY DAMN GUTTED

Results from a survey of 100 flatters.

044

'some people just need **A HIGH FIVE IN THE FACE, WITH A PAN**.'

—

Male, 23
Wellington

TOP TIP

Consider location when flat hunting. Pick a house close to supermarkets and your daily hangouts.

FINDING A FLAT TO RENT

IF YOU'VE DECIDED TO TAKE ON YOUR OWN LEASE, YOU'D BETTER GET READY FOR THE HOUSE HUNT.

So, rather than move into an established flat you're going to go out and find your own place. Great idea! Not only does this mean you can fashion your own flatting world around you, you'll learn all sorts of new skills from all the leg work, paperwork and emotional energy that goes into finding a place of your own.

01

Establish your wish-list

- Before the flat hunt begins, figure out your basic requirements. What are your ideal suburbs, how many bedrooms do you need, how much rent can you afford?

- If you are moving in with others, consult them—what's on their list of must-haves?

- Work out what you can compromise on, because chances are you'll have to.

02

Where to look

- Start with your social network—friends, family and workmates. They may know of a place coming up for rent. Check on local noticeboards, and in the TO RENT column of the local newspaper.

- Check out the rental section on Trade Me and other house listing sites such as nzflatmates. The search tools on these sites make short work of narrowing down your options.

03

Get ready to roll

- The early bird catches the worm. Arrange to view the property as soon as possible.

- If you are going to have flatmates, work together as a team—you're much more likely to succeed if everyone gets involved in the flat hunt.

- Be prepared for multiple flat viewings—chances are you won't find the right place first time. Or even second. Or maybe even third.

04

Check it out

- Don't go alone if it can be avoided—make sure at least two flatmates view the flat together.

- Make a good impression by turning up on time, dressed well, with your best manners turned on.

- If you don't like the flat you are viewing, tell them you appreciate them showing you around and you will get back to them if you still require a flat.

05

Put your best foot forward

- Fill out any necessary paperwork promptly and carefully to get a head start on other applicants.

- It's not a good idea to lie about your name, age, job, or income, but it may pay to stretch the truth about how clean, tidy and responsible you are.

- Have references ready, as is it highly likely that you'll be asked for them. Warn your referees ahead of time, so they have a chance to make up a few stories.

06

If at first you don't succeed…

- Try not to get discouraged if you struggle to find flats that you like, or miss out on them when you find them. In many locations the flat market is fiercely competitive, so you'll just have to be persistent.

- If you're presenting yourself well, filling in applications correctly, and have good references but still not having any luck, consider tweaking your approach. Perhaps you need impress upon the prospective landlord that you're very keen on gardening?

ts.co.nz

...E, ...woman late ...live in J'ville & would like to share expenses with woman in similar employment & single status, pls ring/text 0212541238

FLATMATES WANTED

HATAITAI. dbl rm avail in spacious, sunny hse. Share with 2 females (aged 28 & 33). Call/Txt Kate 021...

A PROF C...
Massage

HK PROFESS...
town. 12-9pm

HOT OIL HEA...
HIGH ST LH 58...

New Healthy Ma...
Japanese/China Ph...

TEND...

FLATMATE WANTED
MUST BE HOUSE-TRAINED
AND NOT A NUT JOB PLEASE

—

Male, 23
Wellington

FLAT-MATES WANT-ED

FINDING A GOOD FLATMATE TAKES LUCK, SKILL AND THEN SOME.

'ALL FIVE OF MY FLATMATES ARE PERFECT IN EVERY WAY.'

—

No one ever

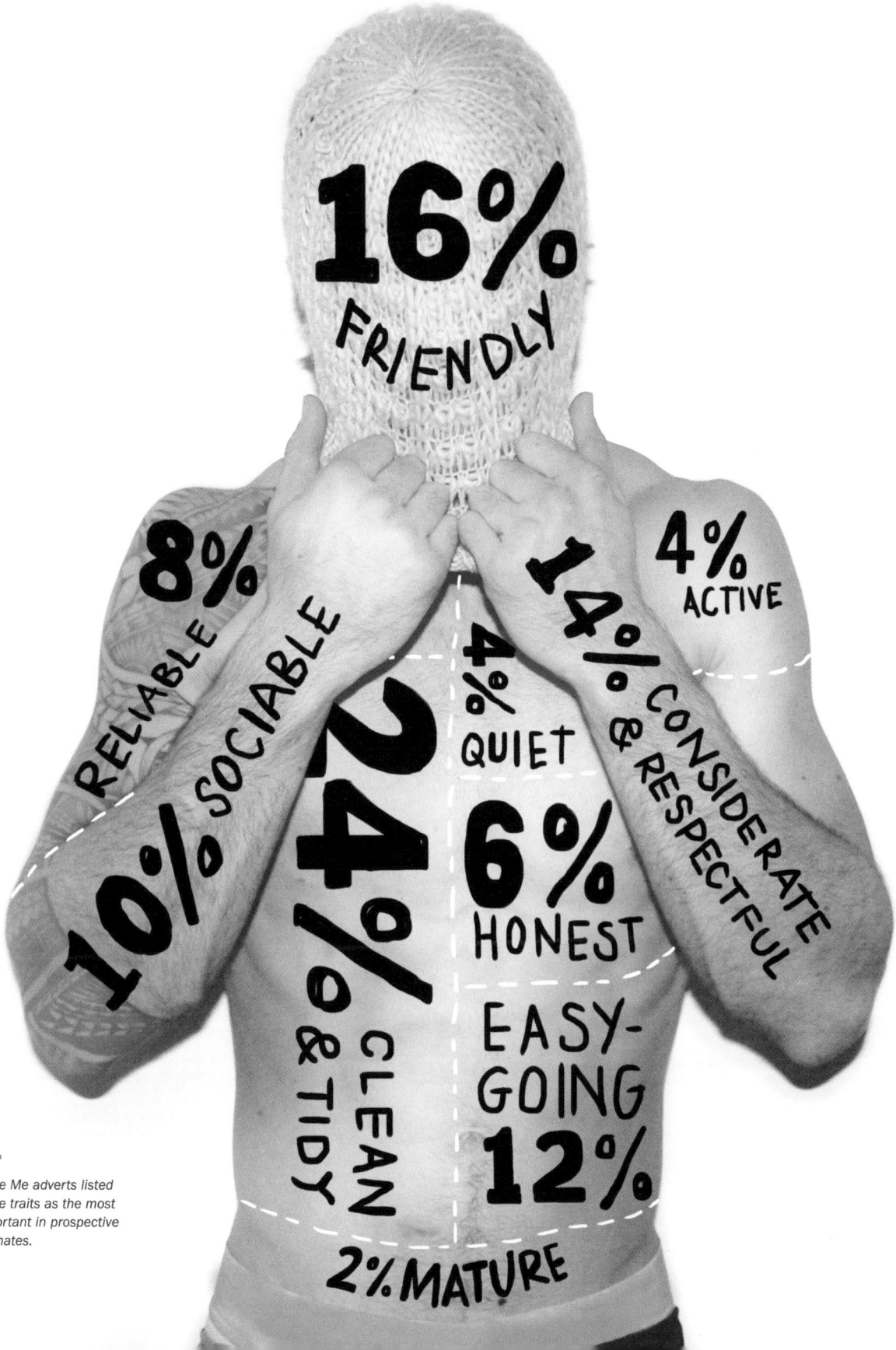

16% FRIENDLY

8% RELIABLE

10% SOCIABLE

4% ACTIVE

14% CONSIDERATE & RESPECTFUL

4% QUIET

6% HONEST

24% CLEAN & TIDY

EASY-GOING 12%

2% MATURE

Trade Me adverts listed these traits as the most important in prospective flatmates.

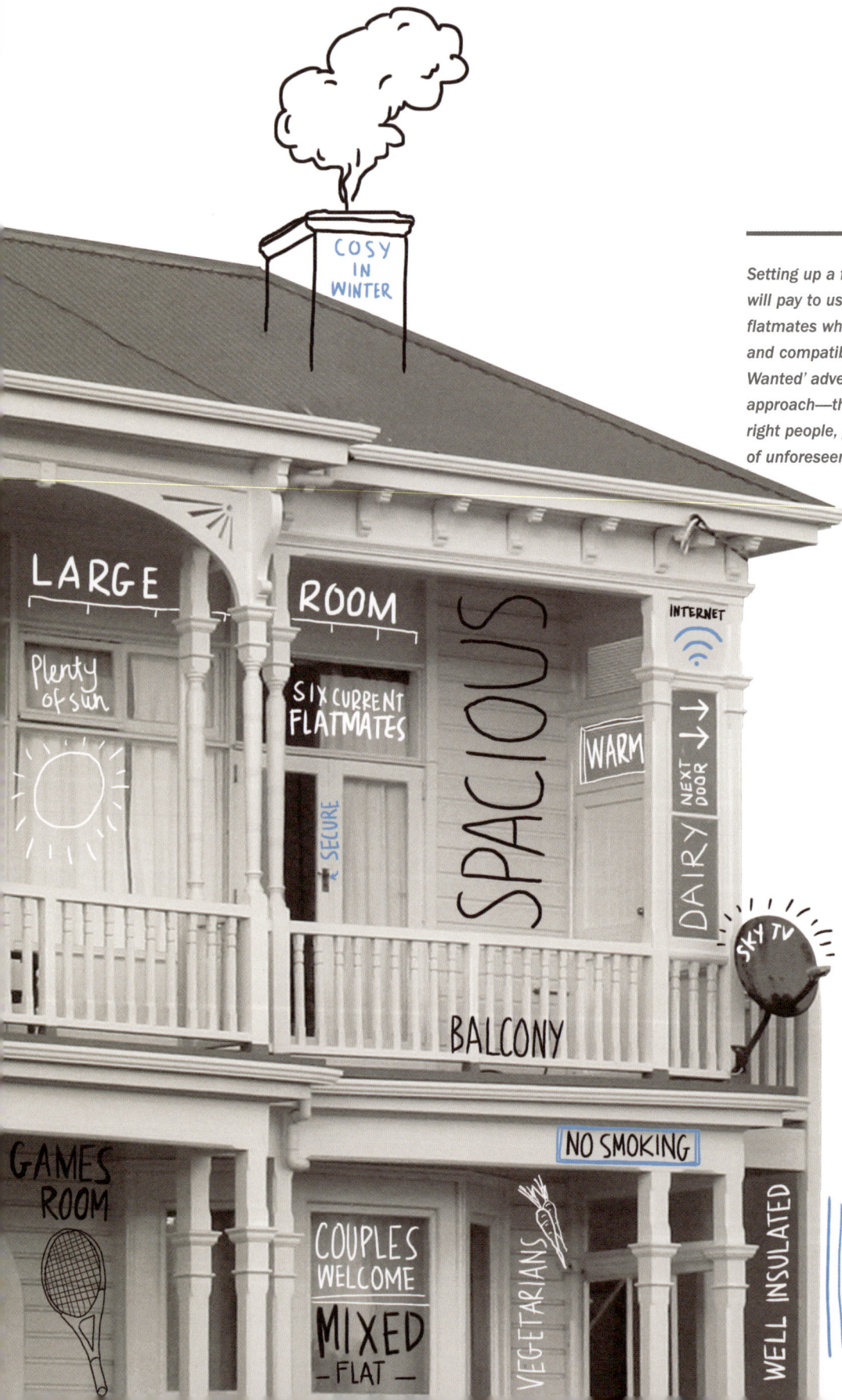

COSY IN WINTER

Setting up a flat isn't brain surgery, but it will pay to use your grey matter to select flatmates who are responsible, reliable, and compatible. Before posting 'Flatmate Wanted' adverts, carefully consider your approach—the right ad will attract the right people, potentially saving you a lot of unforeseen problems.

LARGE ROOM

SPACIOUS

Plenty of sun

SIX CURRENT FLATMATES

& SECURE

WARM

INTERNET

DAIRY NEXT DOOR →↓

SKY TV

BALCONY

NO SMOKING

GAMES ROOM

COUPLES WELCOME

MIXED — FLAT —

VEGETARIANS

WELL INSULATED

Where to advertise

There are endless places to advertise for flatmates, but keeping it local is usually your best bet. Word of mouth is a powerful medium, and often attracts friends of friends who can be vouched for by people you trust—if they like this person, you probably will too. Consider placing adverts in places you go, such as bulletin boards at university or your workplace, or in coffee shops and other local hangouts. All of these options are free. To cast the net wider, consider paid advertising in newspapers, magazines, or websites—media that you personally read. Where you advertise will have a significant bearing on who responds.

It's all about you!

Describing yourself and your situation often proves more fruitful than seeking a perfect match to your 'ideal flatmate' profile. For a starter, your ideal flatmate probably doesn't exist, although you may get people who will fake it just to make the right impression. It's much better to encourage applicants to self-screen according to your living arrangements. If you're seeking a flatmate quite like you, highlight the features in the house that drew you to it. The people interested in this type of living should be reasonably compatible with you.

Include in your ad

An engaging headline
Catch the attention of the right people with a targeted headline that is straight to the point. For example, if you'd prefer a fellow university student, you could write: 'Flatmate wanted to share great apartment near Massey.'

Location & room size
For most flat-hunters, location is critical, so state this upfront and give an idea of how far it is to walk to a popular landmark. Protect your privacy by including only the street name or apartment building, not the specific number or unit. Indicate whether the room is small or large, and whether a couple is welcome. Mention any furnishings, storage or defining features such as a view or all-day sun.

A feel for the place
Give readers an idea of the flatting situation. Outline the make-up of the flat (two males, one female), and use words that best describe the vibe, whether it be 'chilled', 'sociable', 'quiet', or 'warm'. List key features such as a sunny patio, games room or garage.

Rent & extras
Be clear on weekly rental costs along with any extras such as power, internet and Sky TV.

Essential attributes
The whole point of the advertisement is to attract the right sort of person, so if you want a non-smoker, say so. If you want someone under 30, say so. Don't be afraid to put it out there: 'fun flatmate wanted', or 'vegetarian preferred'.

Contact details
Include your first name and contact information, but don't include your last name.

TOP TIP

Try to live with people who work similar hours to you. Coming home to an empty house can be lonely.

APARTMENT

FLAT → OR OTHERWISE KNOWN AS

Cav

ACCOMMODATION

SHITHOLE

TIP

Condo

BASE.

DUMP

HOUSING UNIT

PLACE

SHAREHOUSE

ADDRESS

Suite

COOP

LIVING QUARTERS

LOFT

SHED

CHAMBERS

DIGS

DEN

STUDIO

HOUSING

HOME

PENTHOUSE

BACHELOR PAD

Head Quarter

BASE

HABITAT

rental

DUNGEON

CRIB

HOUSE

SANCTUARY

GO-DOWN

PAD

gerbil cage

ROOST

hole in the wall

CASA

DOMICILE

HOOD

RESIDENCE

PIG PEN

Housing unit

HOLE

Bachelorette pad

CO-OP

lodge

LIVING SPACE

HEARTH

DWELLING

Joint

haunt

CRASH PAD

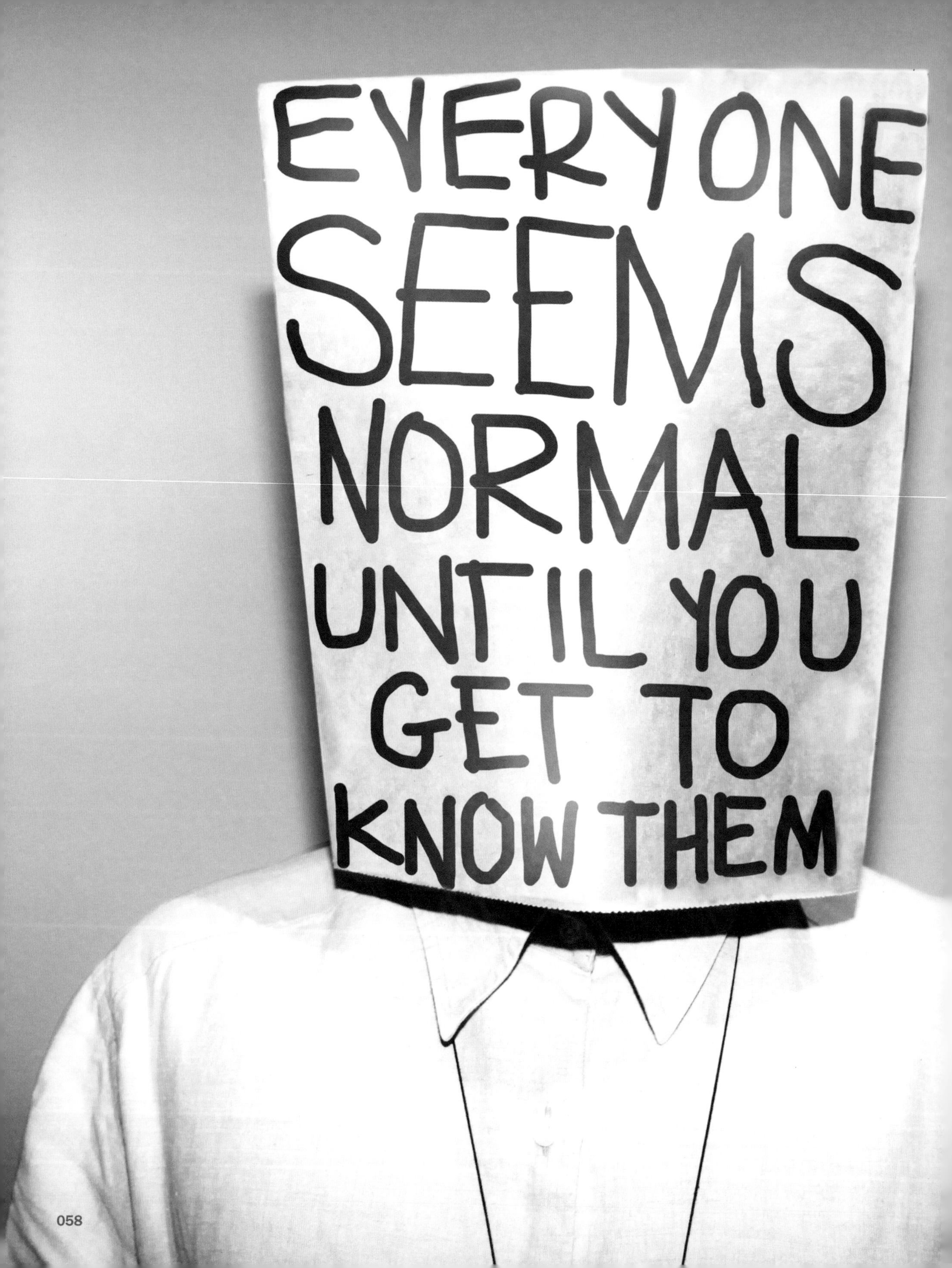
EVERYONE
SEEMS
NORMAL
UNTIL YOU
GET TO
KNOW THEM

INTERVIEW STRATEGIES

QUESTIONS TO ASK PROSPECTIVE FLATMATES

Maybe you like the look of an applicant and they fit your technical specifications (male, non-smoker, quiet type) but how do you really know whether they'll be any good to live with? The answer is, you don't. But start asking questions and you may find the answers reveal more about that person than you expect.

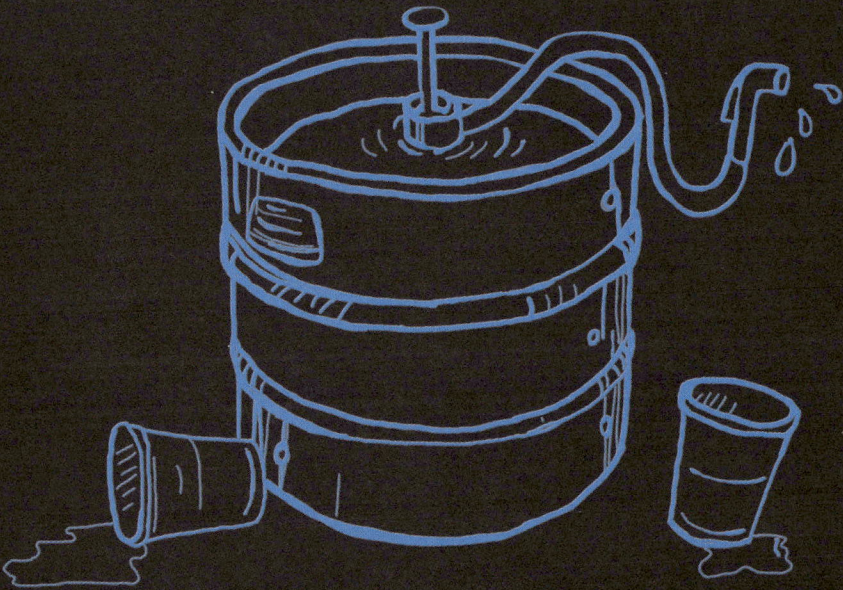

Hi, it's nice to meet you…

How old are you and where are you from?

Is this your first time flatting?
OR
Why are you leaving the flat you're in?

How do you feel about parties or socialising at home?

Do you spend lots of time at home or do you go out regularly?

What kind of music do you listen to?

Do you have any hobbies or play sport?

Do you have any preference for joint groceries and shared meals?

Do you cook, and do you have any special dietary requirements?

What's your attitude to housework?

Will you be bringing any furniture or other large items of property?

What are your long-term plans?

Are you willing to be jointly responsible for paying bills and dealing with the landlord?

TOP TIP

Be sure to debrief properly with your flatmates after the interview. Others may see things differently.

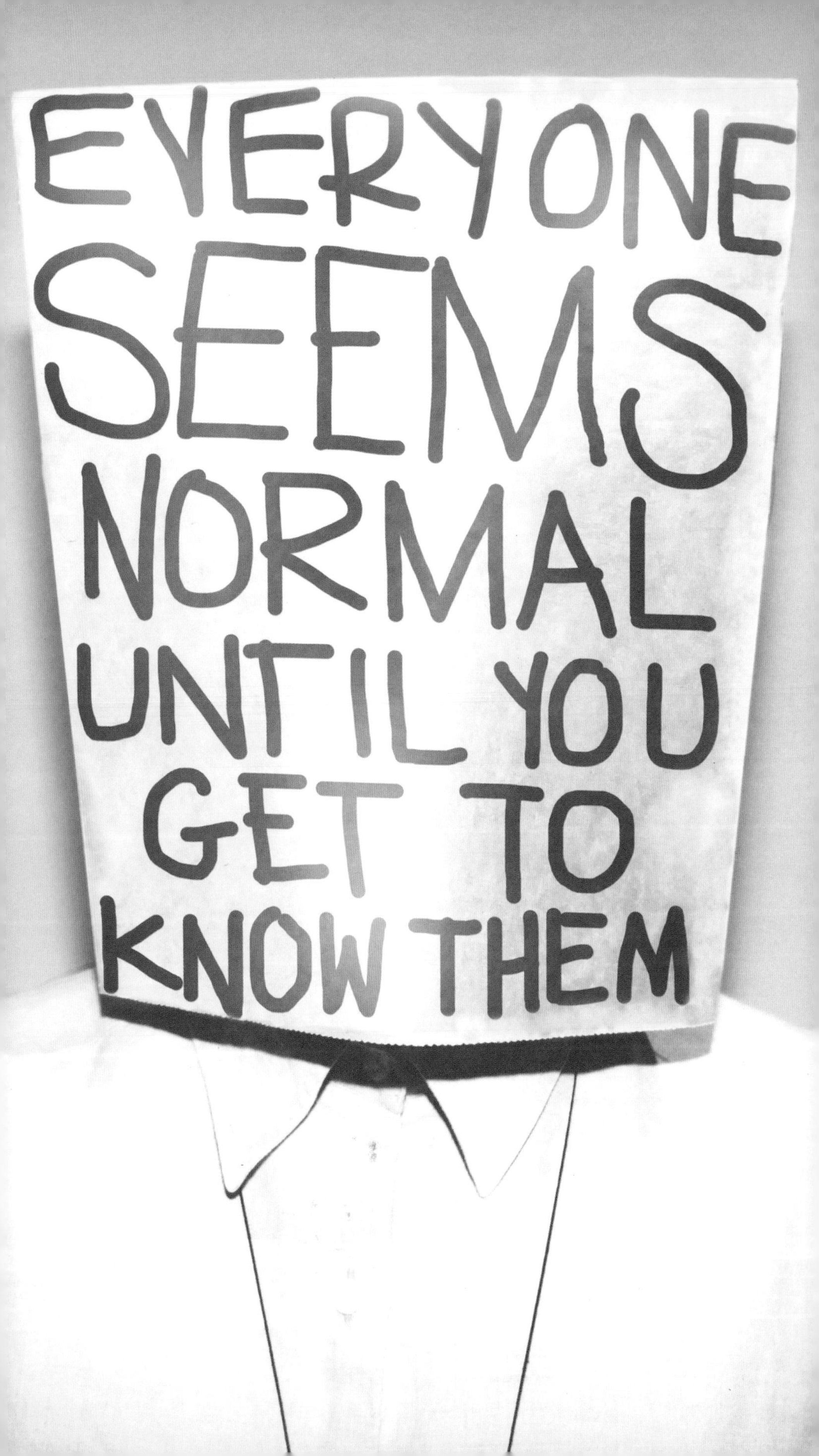
EVERYONE
SEEMS
NORMAL
UNTIL YOU
GET TO
KNOW THEM

TOP TIP

—

Be open-minded about people—but not so much that your brain falls out.

—

'IT'S ONLY WHEN YOU'RE **LIVING IN CLOSE CONTACT** THAT YOU REALISE JUST HOW **WEIRD** AND **WONDERFUL** SOME PEOPLE ARE.' — *Male, 24 Wellington*

GET YOUR CREEP ON

CONDUCT SOME BACKGROUND RESEARCH ON THE APPLICANT

'I RECKON IT'S BEST TO **BE UPFRONT** ABOUT THE FACT THAT I DON'T WANT TO LIVE WITH A NERDY STUDENT OR AN UNEMPLOYED X-BOX ADDICT.'

—

Male, 21
Wellington

Where to look to get the low-down

There's no shame in seeking character references or researching prospective flatmates in other ways—it's likely they'll be doing the same to you. Start by contacting their referees: they should be happy to answer any reasonable questions around reliability and trustworthiness. Facebook is always worth a look, and if you're particularly curious you can dabble with a simple internet search and see what comes up.

Go with your gut instinct

There are no certainties in this game, even if the applicant fronts up with glowing references and flashes the bond. A noticeable 'click' indicates that you've found a suitable flatmate. Conversely, if you feel uneasy about this person, or even just mildly unsure, consider a second interview. It's a lot easier to screen an applicant at the interview stage than to kick them out once they've moved in!

TOP TIP

—

Be prepared to compromise. Your interviewee may not be perfect. The same probably goes for you.

—

SO, YOU'VE FOUND A FLAT AND SOME
FLATMATES. NOW THE FUN BEGINS!
SO DO THE DRAMAS, THE DISH WARS,
AND THE TWO-MINUTE-NOODLE DIET.

FREEDOM

CLEANING UP
OTHER PEOPLE'S MESS

WAKING UP AT **UNGODLY** HOURS OF THE MORNING.

THINGS TO LOOK FORWARD TO

→ SOME FLATTING MOMENTS TO EMBRACE, LEARN FROM AND LOOK FORWARD TO.

COLD SHOWERS

GOING ON THE FATKINS DIET.

BILLS

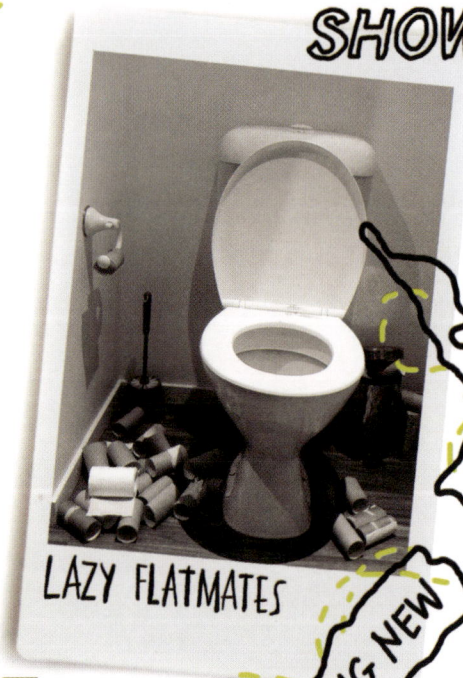

LAZY FLATMATES

MEETING NEW PEOPLE

PEOPLE PEEING IN THE RUBBISH BIN

Strangers showing up and cooking in your kitchen

DISH WARS

DO YOUR DISHES

Making friends

YOUR FLATMATE'S BOYFRIEND EATING YOUR CHEESE

BUDGETING

GETTING EXCITED ABOUT MAKING BREKKY ON WINTER MORNINGS JUST FOR THE CHANCE TO WARM YOUR HANDS OVER THE TOASTER

LAUNDRY AND PLENTY OF IT!!

AFTER HAVING A **PARTY**... FINDING **BEER CAPS** IN THE STRANGEST PLACES FOR WEEKS AFTER —

— THE BREAD MAKER, THE TOILET BRUSH HOLDER IN YOUR BED —

PARENTLESS HOMES

LOUD FLATTIES

INDEPENDENCE

BILLS

FREE

FLEA-RIDDEN FURNITURE

BILLS

LEARNING WHAT YOUR BIGGEST **PET PEEVES** ARE

CHOOS-ING BED-ROOMS

BRILLIANT IDEAS FOR DECIDING WHO GETS WHICH ROOM WITHOUT THE HAIR-PULLING.

'MY FLATMATE WAS A MENTAL CASE. HE **MEASURED** THE ROOMS, INCH FOR INCH AND **DIVIDED** UP THE RENT ACCORDINGLY.' —

Male, 27
Melbourne

01

Size up

Some rooms are better than others, and there will usually be one that is smaller/damper/grosser than the rest. Split the rent accordingly, and you may find the selection process goes quite smoothly.

02

A horse race

Everyone goes out to the TAB and places a bet on a different horse. The order in which the horses come in dictates who gets first dibs.

03

The cook-off

Put your cooking skills to test. Each member of the flat has to cook their best dish. Invite an independent judge to do a blind taste test—best dish, best room.

04

The swap

Swap rooms halfway through your lease. Tip: Shotgun the best room first because when it comes round to swapping time it's likely you will all have forgotten about the agreement!

05

Skittle count

Buy a big bag of Skittles. Each flatmate picks a colour, and then the Skittles are counted by colour. The highest colour counts win. (This competition offers the bonus of eating delicious treats.)

06

Milk skull

Who can finish a two-litre bottle of milk first? Or who can down big bottle of their favourite bevie first? Be aware that you may feel a little queezy after all that liquid.

07

Sperm count

This one is for the fellers: test who has the highest sperm count—highest count, biggest room, lowest count, smallest room!

08

Reward the champion

Sometimes finding a flat in the first place can be a nightmare. The person who puts in the most effort to win the flat could be rewarded with first dibs.

09

Lucky dip

Write everyone's names on pieces of paper and pop them into a hat. Last name left in the hat wins. Easy!

KITTING OUT YOUR FLAT

HOW AND WHERE TO GET FURNITURE AND OTHER FLAT ESSENTIALS.

So you've finally moved in and got your bed made, but when you sit down to watch television you realise you haven't got one, nor a sofa, a fridge, or a bottle opener for the beers. It's time to start hunting down the essentials.

Cheap score

Mention that you're moving into your first flat, and all sorts of free stuff may start popping out of the woodwork—your parents will see it as an excuse to replace their sofa, or a friend will want to get rid of an old dining table. Drop a few hints and see how you go! Your next ports of call are secondhand shops, Trade Me, Freecycle and suchlike where you'll pick up all manner of useful items for a song, the upside of living in a throwaway society.

Buy wisely

Not everything will come free or cheap, so be prepared to shell out for some things. Many small, inexpensive items can be scooped up from cut-price department stores. Regardless, keep an eye out for sales and special hire purchase deals. You may find it's cheaper to pay off a new fridge than it is to hire an old one, especially when you spread the repayments over several years.

TOP TIP

Appliance rentals are a handy short-term solution, but you will pay for this convenience.

HOUSEHOLD GEAR LIST

The Flat Essentials List

Flat essentials

- [ ] fridge/freezer
- [ ] washing machine
- [ ] jug & toaster
- [ ] pots & pans
- [ ] cutlery
- [ ] cooking utensils
- [ ] can/bottle opener
- [ ] crockery
- [ ] glassware
- [ ] cutting board
- [ ] mixing bowls
- [ ] food containers & wrap
- [ ] dining table & chairs
- [ ] sofa/armchairs
- [ ] coffee table
- [ ] tea towels
- [ ] bath mat
- [ ] toilet brush & holder
- [ ] soap & dispenser
- [ ] vacuum cleaner
- [ ] broom
- [ ] mop & bucket
- [ ] cleaning gear
- [ ] clothes-drying rack
- [ ] heater
- [ ] iron & ironing board
- [ ] light bulbs
- [ ] laundry basket & pegs

Flat extras

- [ ] microwave oven
- [ ] television
- [ ] DVD player/movie collection
- [ ] lamps
- [ ] rugs
- [ ] stereo/music
- [ ] bookshelves
- [ ] coffee plunger/stovetop
- [ ] pot plants
- [ ] tool kit (screwdrivers, etc)
- [ ] bathroom scales
- [ ] fan
- [ ] dehumidifier
- [ ] posters, artwork, ornaments

Emergency survival kit

Just because you're young, wild and free doesn't mean you're immune from unforeseen disasters. 'Get Ready, Get Thru' by assembling an emergency survival kit:

- [ ] bottled water
- [ ] long-life food
- [ ] warm clothes
- [ ] wet wipes, soap, toilet paper
- [ ] first-aid kit
- [ ] torch
- [ ] candles
- [ ] batteries
- [ ] gas camp stove
- [ ] can opener
- [ ] disinfectant
- [ ] blankets
- [ ] plastic bags
- [ ] pet food
- [ ] bucket

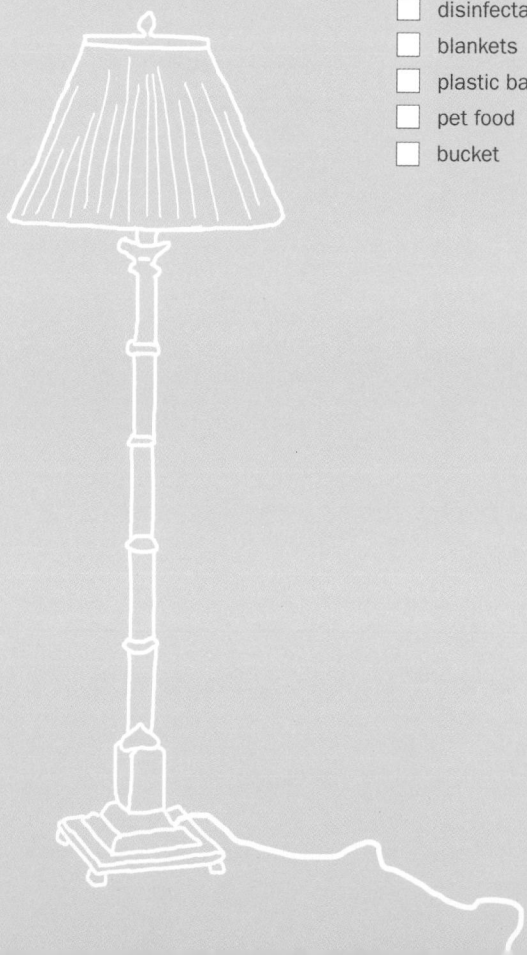

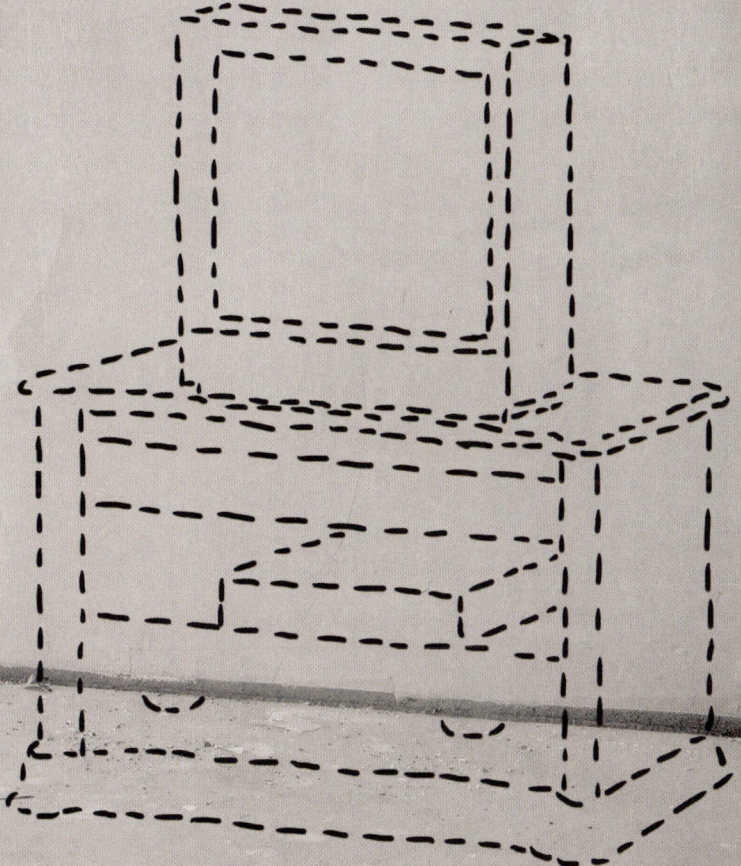

THE HAPPY LAND- LORD

HOW AND WHY YOU
SHOULD BECOME BUDS
WITH YOUR LANDLORD.

'COMMON SENSE IS A FLOWER THAT DOESN'T GROW IN EVERYONE'S GARDEN'. —
*Female, 25
California*

A landlord will place considerable value on a good tenant. From their perspective it is better financially to keep a place responsibly tenanted at a lower rent than it is to face a period of vacancy and run the risk of a bad tenant. Be good, and your landlord may reward you by not putting the rent up, offering retainer rent over summer, and making helpful upgrades as requested. Remember your landlord is not a mind reader! Don't whinge about something being wrong, do nothing about it, and then bring it up when they're chasing you for rent. Let the landlord know as soon as there's a problem so they have the best opportunity to put it right.

Do

- Pay rent promptly and in full.

- Dispose of rubbish responsibly.

- Ask for permission before painting anything or taking down curtains.

- Make sure your landlord can always reach you by phone or email.

- Mow lawns regularly if required.

- Be a good neighbour.

- Turn the bass down.

- Tell your landlord if anything gets damaged or needs fixing.

Don't

- Get into arrears without explaining the situation to your landlord.

- Move a whole bunch of friends in who aren't on the lease.

- Turn the lawn into a muddy mess by parking your car on it.

- Let the backyard turn into a jungle, or a rubbish dump.

- Piss off the neighbours.

- Turn the place into a drug lab.

Know your rights

Your landlord has obligations to you, too. A good landlord will…

- Take care of basic maintenance.

- Pay the rates and house insurance.

- Notify you if they put the house up for sale.

- Give two days' notice of an inspection.

- Do no more than one inspection every four weeks.

- At least listen to any temporary rental problems you might have; ideally they will give you time to sort them.

- Give you ten days' to pay any unpaid rent, and apply to the Tenancy Tribunal should they wish to throw you out.

- Give 60 days' notice before increasing your rent. Rent can only be increased twice a year.

FLATT-ING AGREEMENT

AVOID FLAT TROUBLES BY GETTING EVERYONE ON THE SAME PAGE FROM THE START.

FRIDGE FLOWCHART

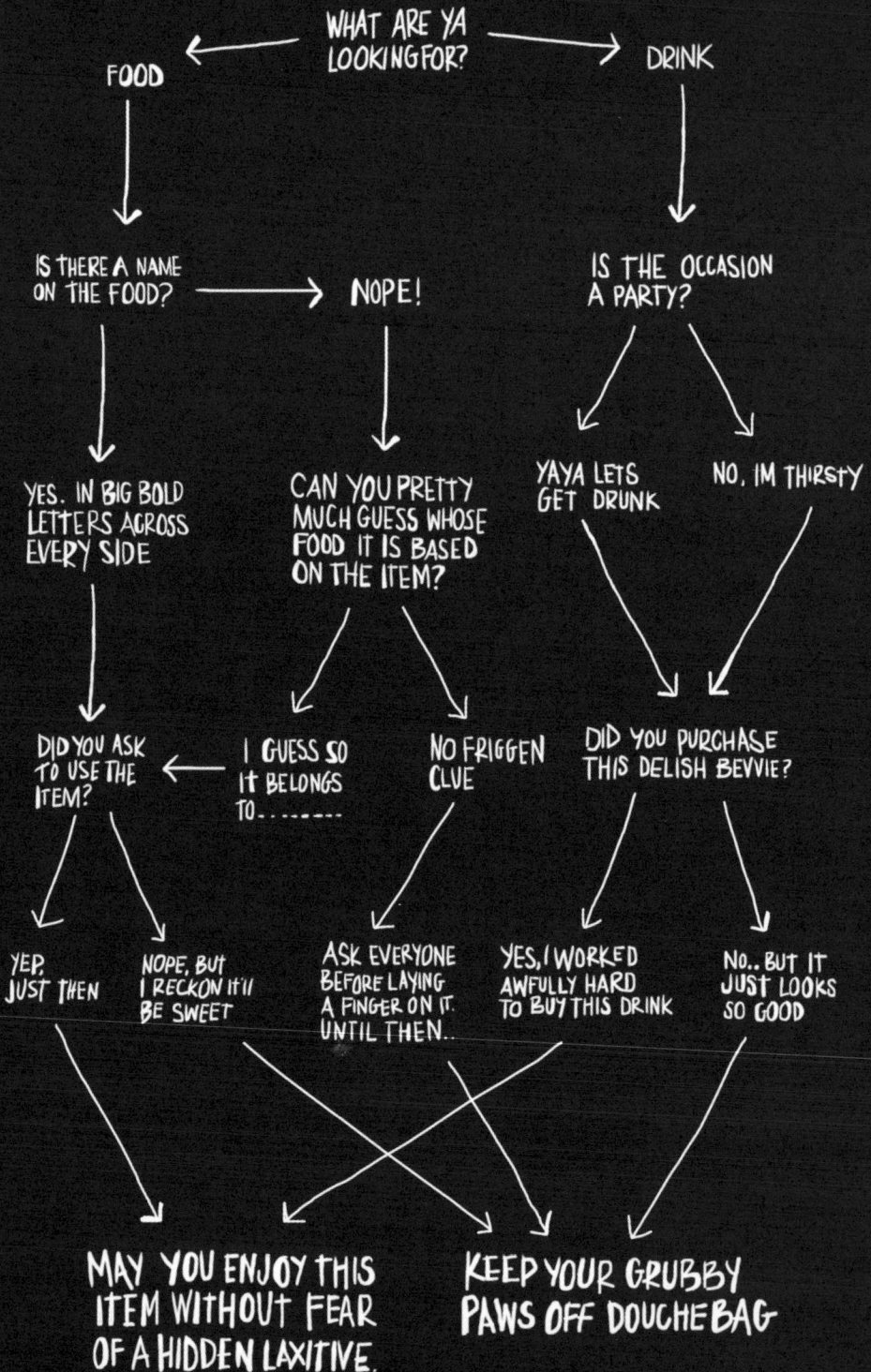

WHAT ARE YA LOOKING FOR?

FOOD

DRINK

IS THERE A NAME ON THE FOOD? → NOPE!

IS THE OCCASION A PARTY?

YES. IN BIG BOLD LETTERS ACROSS EVERY SIDE

CAN YOU PRETTY MUCH GUESS WHOSE FOOD IT IS BASED ON THE ITEM?

YAYA LETS GET DRUNK

NO, IM THIRSTY

DID YOU ASK TO USE THE ITEM? ← I GUESS SO IT BELONGS TO........

NO FRIGGEN CLUE

DID YOU PURCHASE THIS DELISH BEVVIE?

YEP, JUST THEN

NOPE, BUT I RECKON IT'll BE SWEET

ASK EVERYONE BEFORE LAYING A FINGER ON IT. UNTIL THEN..

YES, I WORKED AWFULLY HARD TO BUY THIS DRINK

NO.. BUT IT JUST LOOKS SO GOOD

MAY YOU ENJOY THIS ITEM WITHOUT FEAR OF A HIDDEN LAXITIVE.

KEEP YOUR GRUBBY PAWS OFF DOUCHEBAG

FLAT RULES... DISCUSS!

Being clear on responsibilities and the consequences of not meeting them might seem unnecessary during your flat's honeymoon period. It's only when the wheels start falling off that you'll wish you'd laid down some ground rules. To guard against confusion and hurt feelings, write the rules down. Do this sooner rather than later, because it's a whole lot easier to have these conversations while it's still hypothetical and emotions aren't involved. Make sure everyone in your flat is in on the discussions so they all get their say. Oh, and if you have any pet hates, now is a good time to raise them. Also consider signing a pledge so that rule-breakers can be held accountable.

01

Tenancy agreement & bond

Lease signatories ....

Primary contact with the landlord/letting agent ....

Bond Paid:

| .... | .... | .... |
| Name | Amount | Date paid |

| .... | .... | .... |
| Name | Amount | Date paid |

| .... | .... | .... |
| Name | Amount | Date paid |

02

Rent & bank account

Total rent due ....

Payment frequency ....

Split as follows:

| .... | .... |
| Name | Amount |

| .... | .... |
| Name | Amount |

| .... | .... |
| Name | Amount |

03

Bills

We agree to deposit $ .... each weekly/fortnight/monthly to cover the power, water, telephone and internet. Any underpayment/overpayment will be split equally as required.

The person responsible for the power bill is...

The person responsible for the telephone/internet bill is...

The person responsible for the Sky TV bill is...

The person responsible for the............................... bill is..

04

Telephone/SkyTV

☐ We agree to keep a written record of all toll calls.

OR

☐ We will set up personal pin codes for toll calls.

☐ All flatmates agree to any pay-per-view movies or sports matches.

05

Shopping/Meals

We agree to pay $ .... each week into the flat account to cover shared groceries for daily breakfast and shared meals, as well as for cleaning products, toilet paper etc.

☐ Flatmates will be responsible for buying their own lunches and treats

☐ Under no circumstances will flatmates consume other flatmates' personal food or drink supplies without prior permission.

06

Cleaning

☐ Each member of the flat will take equal responsibility for cleaning.

☐ Cleaning will be completed to a minimum standard as agreed by all flatmates.

☐ The flat/cleaning roster will be adhered to by all flatmates.

07

Leaving the flat

.... weeks' notice must be given in advance of a flatmate moving out.

Finding a replacement flatmate will be the responsibility of:

☐ The person leaving

OR

☐ The remaining flatmates

08

The Pledge

By taking this pledge we are committing to making things happen. Or not happen. It depends on whether it's a good thing or a bad thing. Okay, let's be more specific…

We hereby commit to enjoying our flat life as much as humanly possible. In order to achieve this we pledge to maintain open communication lines with one another. We will not talk behind other flatties' backs, nor complain to their faces without just cause. We will not sweat the small stuff unless it involves cake, beer, boyfriends or girlfriends. We will not screw the crew. We will treat each other as equals until such time as someone has proven themselves to be a dick. We will do our best to contribute to flat harmony, and to enjoy each other's company. We are, after all, in the prime of our lives

Failure to adhere to this pledge will result in the following penalty:

....

....
Name   Signature

....
Name   Signature

....
Name   Signature

....
Name   Signature

....
Name   Signature

....
Name   Signature

....
Name   Signature

....
Date

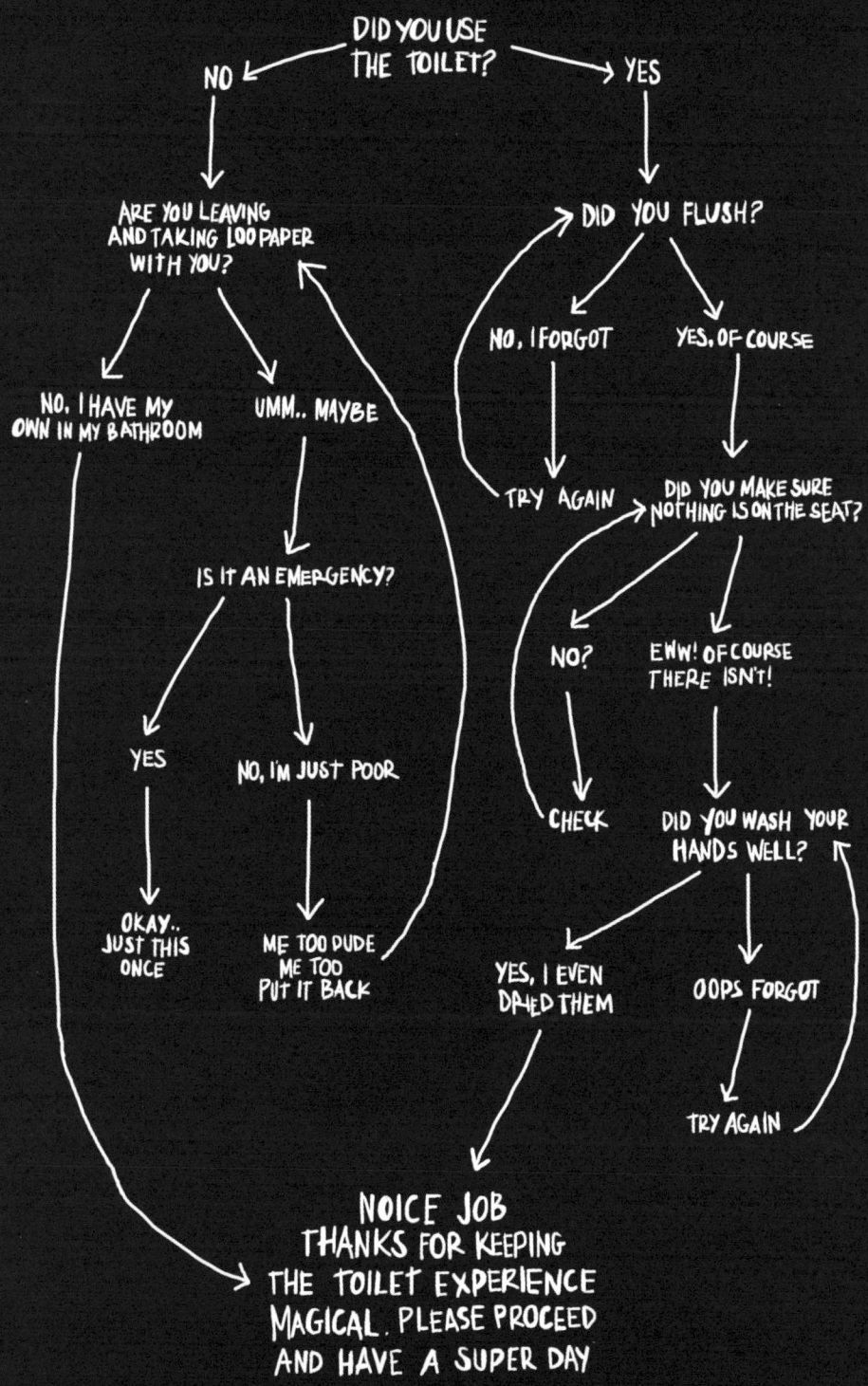

TOILET FLOWCHART

DID YOU USE THE TOILET?

NO

YES

NO →

ARE YOU LEAVING AND TAKING LOO PAPER WITH YOU?

NO, I HAVE MY OWN IN MY BATHROOM

UMM.. MAYBE

IS IT AN EMERGENCY?

YES

NO, I'M JUST POOR

OKAY.. JUST THIS ONCE

ME TOO DUDE ME TOO PUT IT BACK

YES →

DID YOU FLUSH?

NO, I FORGOT

YES, OF COURSE

TRY AGAIN

DID YOU MAKE SURE NOTHING IS ON THE SEAT?

NO?

EWW! OF COURSE THERE ISN'T!

CHECK

DID YOU WASH YOUR HANDS WELL?

YES, I EVEN DRIED THEM

OOPS FORGOT

TRY AGAIN

NOICE JOB
THANKS FOR KEEPING
THE TOILET EXPERIENCE
MAGICAL. PLEASE PROCEED
AND HAVE A SUPER DAY

TOP TIP

—

It's okay to vent. Just be careful whom you vent to.

—

HOUSEHOLD ETIQUETTE

→ COMMON SENSE AND GOOD MANNERS WILL GO A LONG WAY.

IF YOU BORROW IT **RETURN IT**

MITTS OFF!

GRUBBY

KEE

VE RIT

IF SOMEONE IS SLEEPING

BE CONSIDERATE

ZZZZ ZZZZZZZZZ

IF YOU WANT TO BE UNDERSTOOD, EXPLAIN

IF YOU DON'T LIKE SOMETHING

SAY IT!!

IF YOU WANT SOMETHING **ASK**

If you open it, close it.

If you turn it on, turn it off

IF IT DOESN'T CONCERN YOU **DON'T MESS WITH IT**

If you can't fix it, tell someone

IF YOU BREAK IT

FIX IT

IF YOU MOVE IT PUT IT BACK

If you don't know ASK

IF YOU CAN'T READ THIS have someone read it to you.

IF YOU CAN'T HAVE SOMEONE READ IT TO YOU.. YOU'RE F*X*KED

ESTABLISHING BOUNDARIES

I WASN'T STEALING THE FOOD...
I was cleaning the fridge out.

Male, 19
Melbourne

FLAT HARMONY RELIES ON MORE THAN JUST STICKING TO THE RULES.

01
Communal spaces

- Be courteous to other users
- Share it, don't dominate it
- Tidy up after yourself

02
Personal spaces

- Mess up your own as much as you like!
- Respect your flatmates' privacy
- Knock before entering others' rooms

03
Personal property

- Treat others' property as you would your own (in a good way!)
- Ask before you borrow
- Fix or replace any damages

04
Noise

- If in doubt, keep the noise down
- Adhere to any curfew on late-night noise
- Don't clomp around!

05
Food

- Be clear on what are shared supplies, and what are personal
- Consume only your fair share of shared supplies
- Contribute additional supplies, when required
- Replace any 'borrowed' supplies as soon as possible

06
Visitors

- Invite only trusted people into your home
- Ensure everyone is happy with the frequency and number of visitors
- Make sure an appropriate contribution to meals or other costs is offered if necessary

PERSONAL SPACE GUIDELINES

Everyone needs their own space, so don't encroach on others' without consent. Unless you're really close with your flatmates, limit yourself to the social space. There are exceptions for boyfriends, girlfriends, and family, of course.

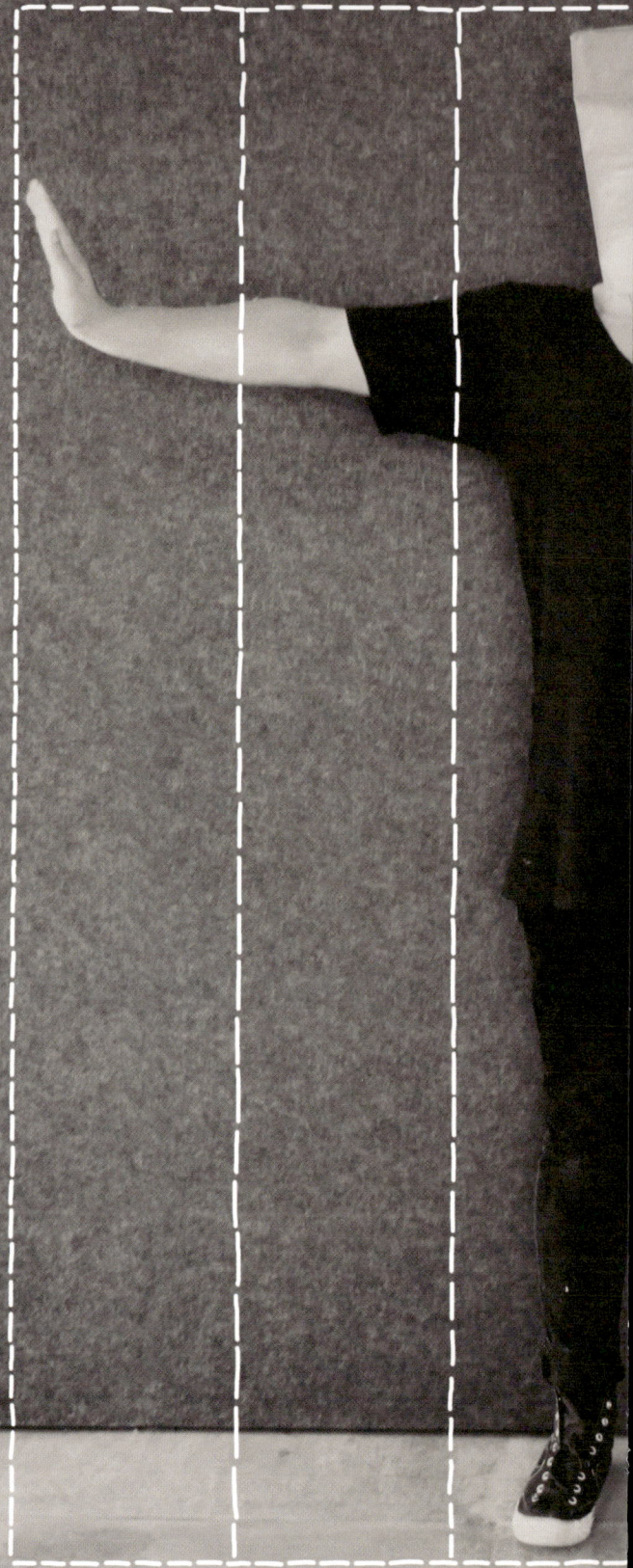

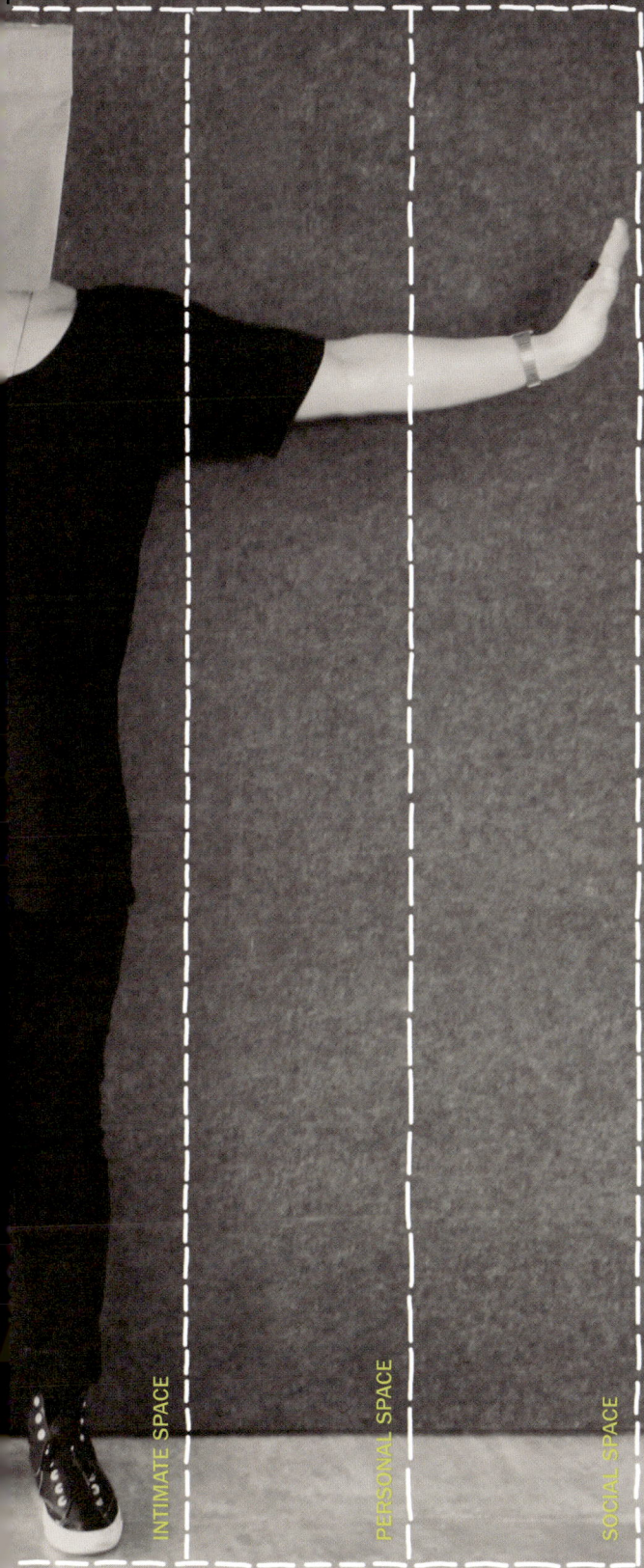

INTIMATE SPACE

PERSONAL SPACE

SOCIAL SPACE

PUBLIC SPACE

Silence is golden
DUCT TAPE IS SILVER

—

Male, 18
Wellington

'STRANGE NEW TREND IN THE FLAT. PEOPLE PUTTING NAMES ON THE FOOD IN THE PANTRY...

TOP TIP

—

Ask before eating other
people's food or using
their things.

—

Today I ate a banana
named Rachel.

—

Male, 20
Auckland

FLAT CHAT—
ARE NOTES OKAY?

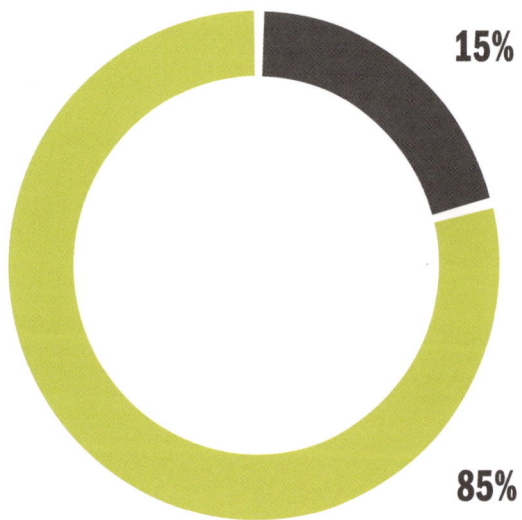

15%

85%

■ YES, BUT ONLY IF THEY ARE FUNNY
■ NO WAY

Results from a survey of 100 flatters.

WHO EVER OWNS THESE
EGGS I GIVE YOU
2 DOLLARS.
I AM DRUNK
THANK YOU FOR
CHICKENS' BABIES

TOP TIP

—

When approaching your
flatmates about any issues,
try to be nice.

—

KEEP-ING IT CLEAN

HARNESS THE POWER OF HOUSEWORK IN YOUR PURSUIT OF FLAT PEACE.

'CLEANING WITH MY FLATTIES IN THE HOUSE IS LIKE BRUSHING MY TEETH WHILE EATING OREOS.'
—
*Male, 28
California*

A dirty flat is bad for your health, especially when your flatmate attacks you with the broom. No one likes a flatmate who doesn't pull their weight when it comes to cleaning. And if that person is you, buck up your ideas, buddy. You're not living with your mother any more.

Who, what & when

It may pay to define and agree on 'clean' at the outset—not everyone has the same standards. Establish who is responsible for cleaning what, and when. A weekly roster or chores wheel may prove a useful reminder for those with short-term memory trouble.

Rubbish & recycling

The rubbish won't bag itself up and take itself out, so take your turn. And perhaps while you're out at the letterbox you might like to pick up that soggy junk mail and that pie wrapper that's been perched in the bushes since your last night on the town.

The bathroom

You know what's unappetising? Other people's toothpaste spittle. Be a pal and give the sink—and vanity top if you're a sprayer—a quick rinse when you're done brushing your fangs. Lads: the same goes for those whiskers you leave behind when you shave. Wash them down the plughole. And you know what's even nastier than other people's toothpaste spittle? Their pee. If you sprinkle when you tinkle, be a sweetie, wipe the seatie.

The kitchen

One day you'll wake up and decide that you no longer want to be the sort of person who engages in passive-aggressive trash wars. (Tactic: smoosh the rubbish down and pull up the sides of the bag in order to convince yourself that the bin isn't full.) Let today be that day! Leaving dishes in the sink temporarily isn't the worst crime in the world. But leaving them for ages is not only nasty but inconsiderate: maybe someone else would like to use that cutting board or cheese grater. Do your dishes. Oh, and you might like to wipe up those crumbs and give the stove a once-over while you're at it.

Your bedroom

If you want to be a slob in the privacy of your own bedroom, go for it! We all have free will and should live the way we want to, as long as it doesn't negatively impact others. So by all means leave that bed unmade, but maybe keep your door shut so your flatmates don't have to see your dirty underwear lying on the floor.

TOP TIP

A visit from friends or family is the perfect excuse for a spring clean.

107

A FLATTER'S CLEANING TIPS

This guide to cleaning will be less than likely to leave your flat gleaming.

Laundry

1. Wash and dry laundry
2. Place in basket
3. Avoid folding
4. Dig through basket all week until out of clean clothes
5. Repeat

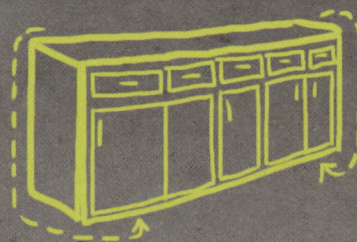

Kitchen benches

1. Sweep crumbs on to floor
2. Kick crumbs under bench

Pet accidents

1. Pretend you didn't see it
2. Run out of the room
3. Wait for someone else to clean it up

Bedroom

1. Realise guests are coming over
2. Close the door so no one sees how you really live

Dishes

1. Place in hot, soapy water
2. Tell yourself they need to soak
3. Go watch TV

COMMON CAUSES OF FLAT DRAMA

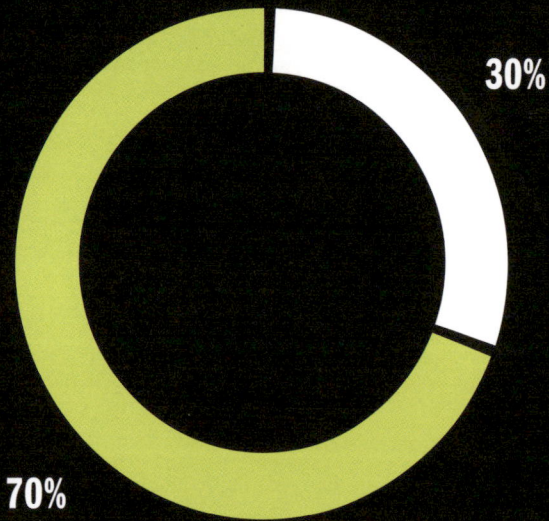

30%

70%

◼ DRAMA CAUSED BY PEOPLE NOT
DOING THEIR DISHES

◼ DRAMA CAUSED BY OTHER ISSUES

*Results from a survey
of 100 flatters.*

'IT APPEARS THAT OUR **ONGOING EXPERIMENT** TO SEE IF THE DISHES WOULD INDEED WASH THEMSELVES HAS ENDED AND ULTIMATELY **FAILED.'** —

Female, 24
Wellington

SOLV- ING CON- FLICTS

CREATIVE WAYS TO DECIDE WHO GETS THE FINAL SAY.

There will be squabbles, you wait and see. They might be over whose turn it is to do the dishes or who gets the last Mallowpuff. They may be over who has to phone the landlord about the broken letterbox. Avoid coming to blows with these suggestions for conflict resolution.

01

Trump card

At the start of the year, every flatmate gets one trump card. This means their decision is final for one argument during the year.

02

Short straws

This childhood favourite is a fitting solution for flatmates who are struggling to behave like adults. It's especially good for arguments that need to be sorted out *fast*.

03

Rock, paper, scissors

Make a quick fist of it with a 'best out of 3'. Don't make it 5, 7 or 9 just because you're losing!

04

Scratch for it

Buy an Instant Kiwi scratchie each. Whoever wins the most money wins the argument (and makes money!). Repeat as desired.

05

Take a nap

You might be over it by the time you wake up.

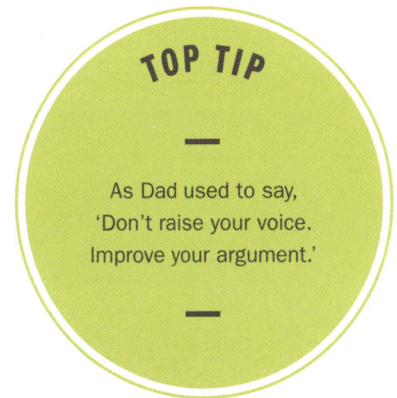

TOP TIP

—

As Dad used to say, 'Don't raise your voice. Improve your argument.'

—

The key is perfecting the art of the smile and nod when all you want to do is PUNCH THEM IN THE FACE

—

Male, 27
Melbourne

114

115

I USE YOUR TOOTHBRUSH

TOP TIP

—

If you're arguing with
your flatmate, be sure to give
your toothbrush a sniff
test before use.

—

WAYS TO MAKE UP FOR BEING A BAD FLATTIE

→ A FEW PROVEN REMEDIES FROM FLATTERS THAT HELP TO MAKE IT RIGHT AFTER BEING A SHIT FLATMATE.

GIVE THEM A LOVING **HUG**

BUY THEM A SIX PACK ...

SCRUB THE LOO AND MAKE IT SPARKLING CLEAN

PICK A GIANT BUNCH OF FLOWERS

SAY YOU'RE SORRY

'SAY SORRY. THEN COOK. THEN CLEAN, THEN GET DRUNK N SAY SORRY AGAIN THEN PARTY AND HOPE ALL WAS FORGOTTEN!'

BRING OUT THE **MAID** IN YOU...

ENSURE THEY GET A GOOD SLEEP

BAKE THEM THESE BAD BOYS. THEY ARE A SURE WINNER.

DOUCHE JAR

THE FAMOUS VANILLA CUPCAKES (SERVES 16)

YOU CAN EVEN FREEZE LEFTOVERS

INGREDIENTS

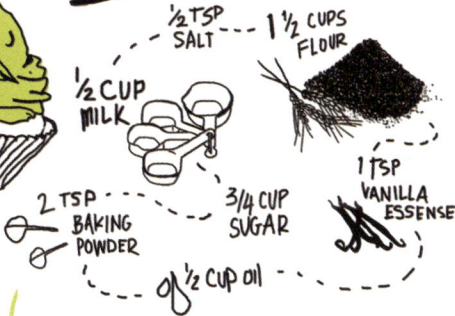

½ TSP SALT

1 ½ CUPS FLOUR

½ CUP MILK

2 TSP BAKING POWDER

3/4 CUP SUGAR

1 TSP VANILLA ESSENSE

½ CUP OIL

METHOD
1. SIFT DRY INGREDIENTS TOGETHER.
2. ADD WET INGREDIENTS TO THE DRY INGREDIENTS.
3. BEAT WELL UNTIL SMOOTH AND CREAMY.
4. PLACE PAPER CUPS INTO TIN AND FILL EACH CUP 3/4 FULL
5. BAKE FOR 15 MINUTES AT 180°C.

ICING
1. CREAM TOGETHER 125g MARGARINE AND 125g ICING SUGAR
2. ADD TWO TABLESPOONS OF MILK AND MIX WELL.
3. ADD COCOA OR FOOD COLOURING.

IF IT'S REALLY REALLY **BAD** YOU MAY NEED TO **MOVE OUT**

—

Deal with any issues straight
away so they don't get worse.

—

I AM THE KIND OF PERSON WHO PREFERS TO **BRUSH SOMETHING UNDER A RUG** AND MOVE ON. MOST OF THE TIME THE RUG STAYS IN PLACE. **BUT** WITH FLATTING, ALCOHOL GETS ON THE RUG, IT GETS THROWN AWAY AND **BOOM** YOU HAVE A SITUATION.

Male, 25
Wellington

121

DOING NOTHING. | IGNORING THE PROBLEM

DEALING WITH FLAT ISSUES

→ HOW PEOPLE COMMONLY DEAL WITH PROBLEMS IN THEIR FLATS.

GETTING THE **HELL** OUT OF THERE

Putting others down —→

DON'T COMMUNICATE VIA POST-ITS.

SERIOUSLY.

Sweet Sweet Revenge

BLOW IT OUT OF PROPORTION

DENIAL

LEAVING NOTES ON EVERYTHING IN SIGHT THAT IS ANNOYING THEM

GETTING REALLY AGGRAVATED

BOTTLING IT UP..

THEN BURSTING

writing anonymous LETTERS

playing nasty

Complaining to other flatties until it finally gets back to the other person through Chinese whispers.

DRAMA

THE BLAME GAME

PASSIVE AGGRESSION

LABELLING THEIR STUFF

BUILD A BRIDGE AND GET OVER IT! ← This method can actually work!!!

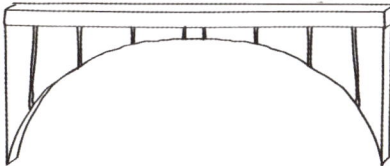

VENTING
TO THE OTHER FLATMATES

Most of these 'resolution' methods don't actually let the person who's bothering you know what's wrong, or what they can do about it. Most people can come up with creative solutions, so long as there is open communication and goodwill. Approach issues as things that need to be worked on together, not as everyone else's problem.

MORE BLOODY GOOD ADVICE

TAKE SOME ADVICE FROM THE PROS ON COMMON FLATTING DILEMMAS.

'SHE ALWAYS BORROWS MY CLOTHES AND 'FORGETS' TO GIVE THEM BACK. I THINK SHE JUST WANTS TO SEE ME NAKED.'
—

Female, 19
Wellington

01

Unwanted guests

Your flatmate's boyfriend is getting a little too comfortable and has pretty much moved in. His toothbrush has its own spot in the bathroom, he drinks all the flat milk and has 30-minute-long showers.

Advice
Discuss boyfriend/girlfriend visitation rights as a flat when you first move in. How many nights per week can they sleep over? Will they put in for bills and food and contribute towards the rent? If so, how much? This doesn't have to be a big deal, just gently but firmly state your rights: who's paying the rent around here?

02

Behind on rent/bills

A flatmate is behind on rent or bills, so you or your other flatmates have to cover it for them. You've made it clear that this can't go on, but they're avoiding the subject and their debt keeps building.

Advice
Prevention is better than cure. A flatmate is less likely to get into arrears if their name appears on the rental agreement or power account, so try to ensure shared responsibility for the flat financials. Make sure any deposits into the flat account are clearly named so it's easy to work out who has paid and who hasn't. Keep an eye on all payments, and nip any lapses in the bud. Approach the non-payer as a united front, and if they repeatedly blow their chances kick them out—do it sooner rather than later to minimise your losses.

03

Noise wars

You're sick, or studying, or just need some peace and quiet, but others are blasting the stereo, stomping around or having rowdy sex. When confronted, they blame paper-thin walls and protest that it's their flat too and they've got as much right to make a ruckus as you have to enjoy silence.

Advice
Clear communication and mutual consideration are your best weapons. Express your views calmly in the hope they will do the same. Perhaps you could agree to quiet periods—certain times of the day, or days of the week—and establish a curfew. Failing that, try earplugs.

PEOPLE WHO NEVER LEAVE

04

Stoner trouble

Your flatties enjoy their fair share of weed. There is a constant grassy stench, the cookie jar is empty, and you're worried about the element being left on and the place burning down.

Advice

It's perfectly reasonable to establish ground rules around smoking, alcohol, and drugs. A total ban isn't the only way to go—you could permit certain activities in particular areas of the property at different times. Ensure your personal insurance policy covers all bases, just in case the flat does in fact burn down. Note: it's best to steer clear of burning the flat down.

05

Electricity hog

The flat's freezing, so you're waddling around in a sleeping bag with your feet hanging out the bottom. Your flatmate, however, is nice and toasty in their bedroom, blasting their fan heater and creating a tropical paradise.

Advice

Before you get snarky remember that not everyone has been taught to conserve power. Address this inequality by pointing out to the electricity hog that the bill is shared, and suggest ways in which they can keep warm (such as eating more pies and wearing snuggly onesies). If they're not prepared to turn the heater down or off, ask them chip in more for the power bill. Fair's fair.

06

Filthy flatties

Dirty is the word that comes to mind when you think of your flatmates. Their bedrooms stink, there are outrageously long pubes stuck to the shower walls and their mountain of dishes is growing.

Advice

When you put a clean freak amongst filthy flatties expect some headbutting. If it becomes evident that flatmates have different tolerances for mess and muck, sort it out quick smart. Agree to a minimum standard, and be clear on penalties for non-compliance. If there is a clean freak in your midst, they should be heavily encouraged to go for gold (but that doesn't necessarily mean everyone else has to!).

You can plan ahead for most of these issues using the flatting agreement, but if worse comes to worst, and gentle persuasion doesn't work, consider asking a neutral outsider to moderate.

SUB-STANDARD COMMUNICATION METHODS

IF YOU USED THE LAST PIECE THROW THIS AWAY AND PUT A NEW ROLL ON

BURNT PIZZA

CHRONIC PARTIERS

CLEANING DILEMMAS

Some challenges that you may come across while flatting.

127

LIVE **CLOSE** TO A GOOD PIE SHOP

BUY IN BULK TO SAVE MONEY

SAVE CASH BY RIDING INSTEAD OF DRIVING

SECRETS OF HAPPY FLATTERS

→ A FEW FUN TIPS FOR CREATING A GREAT LIVING ENVIRONMENT.

BE REALISTIC WITH LEFTOVERS WHEN IN DOUBT THROW IT OUT!

1 · 10 · 2003

clean out the fridge every now and then so you don't end up with nasty suprises . . .

BE MERRY

HAVE FLAT RED CARDS

A SMALL DASH OF BAKING SODA IN YOUR FRIDGE WILL KEEP IT SMELLING FRESH.

BECOME PALS WITH YOUR LANDLORD

— TO AVOID MOULD —
DON'T DRY YOUR CLOTHES IN YOUR ROOM

If you want your
**WHITES
WHITE**
do your washing right!

SEEK INTIMACY
OUTSIDE OF THE
FLATTING SITUATION...

GET YOUR NEIGHBOURS TO LIKE YOU
BEFORE YOUR FLATWARMING

DO ACTIVITIES
AS A FLAT

HAVE FLAT
MOVIE
NIGHTS

BUILD **FORTS**
ON THURSDAYS

Somewhere on your
journey
don't forget
to turn around and
enjoy the view..

EXI
PLA

NOTHING LASTS FOREVER.
THE DAY WILL COME WHEN
IT'S TIME TO MOVE OUT—
THEM, YOU, OR ALL OF YOU.

REPLAC-ING A FLAT-MATE

MAYBE THEY WILL JUMP, OR MAYBE THEY WILL BE PUSHED. EITHER WAY, THEY'RE GOING.

The ideal scenario is that there are no hard feelings and no debts left behind, and that you find a great replacement flatmate quickly and easily so you can start a new chapter in your flat life. Whether this happens or not will largely depend on the circumstances of the departure, personal responsibilities, and the terms and conditions of your lease.

'ONCE YOU HATE SOMEONE EVERYTHING THEY DO IS ANNOYING —LOOK at this hussy eating that carrot like she owns the place.'

Female, 20
Wellington

01

Know your rights

Re-examine any flat agreements and the terms of your lease so you know where you stand. If you suspect things might get contentious, seek advice from someone who has legal knowledge, such as a legal aid officer or lawyer, although an experienced businessperson can probably also help.

02

Be sensitive

Should your flatmate storm out in a tiff, the deed is probably done. On the other hand, any request for them to leave should be handled sensitively and calmly, ideally with all flatmates presenting a united front. The departing flatmate should be free to ask any questions and negotiate the conditions of their exit.

03

Be clear on terms

Negotiate the final leaving date. You may also need to get the lease re-signed, divide any shared property, and conduct a final room inspection.

04

Final bills & bond

Designate a member of the flat to calculate any money owing for rent and bills, or any refunds due from the joint flat account. The flatmate's share of the bond will also need to be returned once it's been ascertained they have met their obligations—that's after the final room inspection and the return of keys.

05

Paperwork

If the departing flatmate is a signatory on the lease, bank account, or utility contracts, you will need to arrange to have these responsibilities reallocated to another member of the flat.

06

Notify the landlord

You are obliged to notify your landlord if a flatmate is moving out. The landlord may also wish to approve the replacement tenant, and have them assigned to the lease.

07

Final room inspection

An inspection of the vacated room should be made before any final bond payment is made. Ensure that the room is left in acceptable condition and that no belongings are left behind.

08

Stopping the gap

Just because one of your rooms is empty for a week or more doesn't mean you're not liable for the rent. However, if you've proven to be good tenants you may be able to negotiate a rent reduction for a short bridging period.

135

YOU'RE LEAVING THE FLAT

FOLLOW THESE SIMPLE STEPS TO ENSURE THE PROCESS OF MOVING OUT RUNS SMOOTHLY.

01
Tell your flatmates

This can be the hardest task of all, especially when you enjoy living with your flatmates and are forced to move due to a change in circumstances. You should tell your household in person, in a group discussion or meeting.

02
Return everything

Make sure you leave any joint household belongings behind, or negotiate to gift, sell or buy them to square things up. Return any personal items that belong to your flatmates, and see they return stuff to you too.

03
Clean up

Clean your room thoroughly before the final room inspection. The more effort you make, the more likely you are to get your bond money back. It's also polite to clean up any of your personal mess in communal areas.

04
Stick around

Attend the final room inspection and make sure that the appropriate documentation is signed off.

05
Take snaps

Take photos of your room after the final inspection—especially of anything you think might be contentious—in case of any future disputes.

06
Walk out even

Pay any outstanding debts and collect any money owed to you including prepaid rent, expenses and bond.

07
Sign out

It may be appropriate to receive a signed discharge letter that states the date you moved out, monies paid and received, and the results of your final room inspection. Return keys to the nominated flatmate or landlord.

08
Tie up loose ends

Contact the utility companies and set the date to turn off or transfer any utilities accounts that are in your name.

TOP TIP

Clean the flat thoroughly to increase the chances of getting your bond back.

I FIND IT HELPS TO ORGANISE
CHORES INTO CATEGORIES:
THINGS I WON'T DO NOW,
THINGS I WON'T DO LATER,
AND THINGS I WILL NEVER DO.

—
Female, 22
Wellington

GET RID OF THE EVID-ENCE

GET READY FOR THE FLAT INSPECTION AND WALK AWAY WITH A FULL BOND REFUND.

01

Your bedroom

If you have carpet, treat any stains as best you can, and vacuum thoroughly. Mop any wooden or vinyl floors. Wipe down shelves, skirting boards and other surfaces. Remove cobwebs, wash the windows and clean the mirrors.

02

Bathrooms

Toilet, bath & shower
Give these a proper scrub-down, removing any built-up scum. Shine up the fixtures.

Vanity & mirror
Clean the mirrors, medicine cabinet and any vents or light fixtures.

Floor
Sweep and mop the bathroom floor. Be especially careful around the toilet.

03

Common areas

Walls
Remove all staples and nails you have stuck into the walls, ceilings or doors. Where appropriate, wash down the walls. Well executed paint touch-ups may be a good idea where major scuffs have appeared.

Windows & blinds
Clean the windows, as well as the frames and sills. Wipe down blinds and wash curtains.

Floors
Spot treat any marks on the carpet and vacuum thoroughly. Mop any wooden or vinyl floors.

Other surfaces
Brush away cobwebs. Wipe ceiling fans, skirting boards, and suchlike.

'SOMETIMES I WRITE DOWN TASKS AFTER I'VE DONE THEM, JUST TO GET THE SATISFACTION OF CROSSING THEM OFF MY LIST.'

Male, 27
Melbourne

04

Outside areas

Balcony, patio & driveway

Sweep any outside areas, and wash down any grubby walls or fences. Pick up any bottles, cigarette butts and other litter. Pull up any epic weeds.

Rubbish

Remove any rubbish and put the rubbish and recycling out for collection. Dispose of any large items, such as that old microwave sitting by the back door.

05

The kitchen

Fridge

If the fridge came with the flat then you should give that a good clean, which includes removing all the shelves and drawers and washing them properly.

Oven

It's a dirty job but someone's gotta do it. You will need a decent spray cleaner, decent tough scourers and elbow grease. When you clean the stove top, remove and clean any gas grates or element rings and give them a good going over. Wipe down that greasy rangehood while you're at it! The whole thing should gleam.

Cupboards & pantry

Make sure all the cupboards are empty and clean for the next tenant. Wipe the shelves.

Sink

Scrub the sink and shine up the taps. Use an old toothbrush for de-griming the fiddly bits.

Other surfaces

Wipe down the outside of the fridge and the dishwasher, clean the microwave inside and out, and shine up any other appliance provided by the landlord.

Floor

Do this job properly by pulling out the stove and refrigerator and cleaning behind them. As well as coming across all kinds of gross stuff on the sides of the appliances and cabinets, you may discover that thing you lost five months ago—it rolled under the fridge.

THE AFTER PARTY

TOP TIP

—

Go to your move-out inspection.
Be sure to get a copy of
the report for your records.

—

THE END

PLEASE STOP STEALING FOOD

I spit IN MINE

NO JOKE

ATTN BRAD
MY PARENTS
ARE COMING
TODAY SO CAN
YOU PLEASE
WEAR PANTS?
TA, FREYA.

YOU HAVE BEEN
SEEN USING
MY BUTTER.
PUT IT BACK OR I WILL
LICK EVERYTHING.

hey hotstuff!
you sure are looking good today!
why not keep the sinks clean
so they can look as gorgeous
as you? YAY Vanity. (get it? Vanity?)
love your bathroom mirror.

DEAR FLATMATES
I KNOW YOU HAVE A HABIT
OF EATING MY FOOD.
PLEASE DON'T BE DISTURBED
BY THE CONTAINER SAYING 'POISON'.
JUST GO AHEAD AND
DO YOUR THING.

DEAR MILK THIEF
THAT WAS BREAST MILK

DUDE YOU PEED IN THE
RUBBISH BIN. THE BATHROOM
RUBBISH BIN. WHY?! YOU WERE
SO CLOSE TO THE TOILET.

all clean -sorry for
my drunkenness.

A GREAT BIG THANK YOU VERY MUCH

I would like to thank everyone for their help in producing this book. First of all, everyone who shared their flatting experiences and offered advice for people going flatting. Also Dayma for his fantastic photography skills. To all the people who welcomed me into their flats to observe and take photos of them. To London, Annette and Anna for their helpful advice and feedback, all the people who feature in this book, the wonderful team at Awa Press and of course to Andy, my friends and family for their ongoing support and encouragement over the past few years. Thank you all very much again.

MORE GUFF

First Time Flatter's Guide: Tips to get you sorted; www.massey.ac.nz; Massey University Accommodation Services

Flatwithme; www.flatwithme.com.au/share-accommodation-resources.html

Sorted: Your Independent Money Guide, www.sorted.org.nz

Flatting; Otago University Students' Association; www.ousa.org.nz/support/flatting/

Flatting 101: Your guide to flatting; www.dbh.govt.nz/flatting-101; Ministry of Business, Innovation and Employment

NZ Flatmates; www.nzflatmates

Private Renting; www.canterbury.ac.nz/accom/flatting/; University of Canterbury

Trade Me – flatmates wanted; www.trademe.co.nz/flatmates-wanted

CREDITS

All photographs were taken by Lauren Earl with the exception of the following:

Author photo – Mahana Vardey

Newspaper room photo – Tamati Turnbull

Contents page, 09 (top right & bottom right), 10 (bottom left), 16, 18–19, 26–27, 32 (left), 36–37, 42–43, 46–47, 50–51, 58–59, 62–63, 67, 84–85, 94–95, 96–97, 102–103, 104–105, 108–109, 114–115, 116–117, 119 (bottom), 120–121, 125, 127 (bottom left), 128–129, 134–135, 138–139, 143 – Dayma Otene

20–21, 24–25 – Max Wong

32–33 (centre) – Dmitry Zubarev, photos.com

64–65 – Chris Searl

76–77, 80–81 – Matthieu Gafsou

10 (far left), 71 (top right), 74–75 – The author and publisher have made all reasonable attempts to contact copyright holders.

AWA PRESS

Award-winning publishers of intelligent,
thought-provoking non-fiction

Read more at www.awapress.com

Follow us on Twitter @AwaPress

Check us out on Facebook/AwaPressNZ

First edition published in 2013 by Awa Press, Level Three,
11 Vivian Street, Wellington, New Zealand.

National Library of New Zealand Cataloguing-in-Publication Data
Earl, Lauren.
Flatter's survival guide / Lauren Earl.
ISBN 978-1-877551-89-5
1. Apartment dwellers—New Zealand—Handbooks, manuals, etc. 2. Apartment
dwellers—New Zealand—Anecdotes. 3. Apartments—New Zealand—Anecdotes.
4. Roommates—New Zealand—Anecdotes. 5. New Zealand wit and humor.
I. Title.643.27092293—dc 23

Cover & internal illustration & design by Lauren Earl
Printed by Midas Printing International Ltd, China

This book is typeset in ITC Franklin Gothic

USE FACEBOOK TO GET YOUR MESSAGE ACROSS. PULL YOUR WEIGHT WITH CL

LATMATES RESPECT YOU AND MAYBE EVEN RETURN THE FAVOUR

ake sure everyone is on the same page when you move in to avoid any nasty suprises

TAKE AN ANNOYING SITUATION AND TRY TO LAUGH IT OFF

agree on a set amount for bills each week.

Be mindful of personal space.

LEARN TO CHANGE A LIGHTBULB

ASSESS THE IMPORTANC OF EACH DRAMA, IS IT W

CHOOSE YOU FLATMATES WISELY

DON'T HAVE SEXY TIME IN YOUR FLATTIES BED!

DON'T PEE IN THE KITCHEN SINK

RELAX A LITTLE

meet flatma movin

earn the basics of cooking so you can fend for yourself.

AT SOME POINT ON YOUR JOURNEY, DON'T FORGET TO TURN AROUND AND ENJOY THE VIEW.

DON'T BE A JERK

TAKE A B FROM THE FL

N'T ALWAYS BRING THE PARTY HOME

T GETS OLD FAST

SPEAK YOUR MIND

YOU ARE HA A SHIT TIM

ont lend money if you are a tight wanker because chances are you won't get it back.

MAKE SURE EVERYONE THE FLATTING AGREEMENT START TO SAVE THE DRAMA

YOU ARE MOVING OUT, LET YOUR latties HAVE A SAY IN WHO REPLACES THEY HAVE TO LIVE THEM.

ENSURE EVERYONE HA ACCESS TO THE FLAT A